ROZ'
LITTLE
MANUAL
FOR
SURVIVING
POTHOLES

Rosalind W. Johnson

authorHOUSE®

AuthorHouse™ LLC
1663 Liberty Drive
Bloomington, IN 47403
www.authorhouse.com
Phone: 1-800-839-8640

Published by AuthorHouse 04/15/2014

ISBN: 978-1-4918-4242-3 (sc)
ISBN: 978-1-4918-4243-0 (e)

Library of Congress Control Number: 2014900568

Also by Rosalind W. Johnson
Friends To Die For
Secret Lives

Coming Soon
T.J. Sloan

Acknowledgements

I am deeply indebted to my editor, Judy Gitenstein for her patience and insight. This little manual could not have been completed without her excellent assistance. My appreciation to the team for their continued encouragement is immense.

This manual is dedicated to all my readers who believe in me and support my continued literary efforts, and to all of you who are pursuing your individual goals and dreams.

It is my hope this little manual will guide your actions to live a more bountiful life as you make the changes necessary to develop your goals, dreams and plans. Most of what is included in this manual is common sense, universal laws, mother wit, ideas your teachers taught or principles you discovered on your own. It is just a reminder I created for easy reference.

—Roz—

When change knocks
on the front door
Fear leaves by the back door
Old habits jump through
the bedroom window
Tired thoughts hide in the closet
Then change comes in, takes its place
and
Sits in the big chair

__Introduction__

Your soul stirring goal to live a full and bountiful life is a journey of change. As with any journey, in addition to the smooth stretches, expect bumpy patches, potholes and hills that often seem more like mountains. Because this journey is powered by your life's purpose, you must have a roadmap of skills to get you around the bumps and potholes. This little manual lays out the five keys to goal achievement by suggesting time-honored skills that never fail. I challenge you to develop and use them. Your journey begins when your goal walks out to meet a **plan**. They pick up **commitment** and **focus**. The three of them coax **discipline** to join this march. Immediately **perseverance** jumps on board. Next stop success.

This manual is relevant no matter your stage in life and the goals you set. In addition to your personal goals, you have goals for your children, grandchildren, family members, professional colleagues, your organizations and communities. This is not a manual about positive thinking nor is it a secret formula for success. It is a guide that transforms your thinking and actions by assisting you in identifying and developing reliable skills that lead to success. Its greatest value is getting you through the hard times you will inevitably experience in meeting your goals and dreams. Even though you may use the words goals and dreams interchangeably to indicate your desire for a particular outcome, the skills needed to manifest the result are unchanged. Take a careful look at the suggested skills and personal actions. Study them. You'll find their logic and scope liberating. They work for small everyday goals as well as your large life goals. You may begin your journey to goal achievement with old habits, but adopting and using the skills recommended in this manual, you arrive with a changed outlook and new behaviors.

Successfully navigating this process we call life is doable. I looked over my own life and discerned what worked in helping me accomplish the goals I set for myself and also discovered the traps that caused me, at times, to fall short. Once I distilled the essence of these skills I observed others, people I considered masters of setting and achieving goals. They believed in themselves and viewed the world with optimism and hope which expanded their opportunities and propelled them forward. Every one of them formulated a plan and persevered to successful conclusion. They stayed the course even through tough days.

There is no mystery to success in the pursuit of goals and dreams. You're born with the tools to direct your destiny and free will to choose. However, before you reach any of your goals, you need to overcome challenges during the journey. Skills and methods discussed here are designed to help you meet these challenges. Many of the skills overlap and interconnect every step of your journey.

In this little manual when I speak of success, I'm referencing more than financial success. It's about exercising control over your life events and enjoying the ride. This guarantees a measure of peace of mind. Explore your capabilities and resources in finding the roadmap to success. The price of goal achievement is time linked to patience, risk and a willingness to stretch beyond your comfort level and current circumstances. Time, like money, is a free agent. Its nature is to work hard only for the person who shows it respect.

There is no guarantee that anything in life is without hard work or struggle, but you can minimize these potholes and bumps in the road by having a clear vision for your goals, developing a plan and acquiring skills necessary to make the vision a reality. The road to goal attainment is a journey in which you must have a plan, be committed to it, focused, disciplined and adopt a never-give-up attitude. Choice and decision making are the common themes of your journey.

No one can take the journey for you. It is your walk. Own your goals and dreams and when you do, you'll take responsibility for their fulfillment. Personal responsibility causes you to think differently. You become more creative in planning and recognize additional opportunities that link necessary information for problem solving. Believe, without a doubt, the direction of your life is yours to determine. Whatever your age, you can change direction, if necessary and reinvent yourself. This may be difficult to understand, because life experiences may have left you feeling powerless, with little or no confidence in the ability to control your own circumstances. Your dreams did not vanish: they still flicker with hope. You can begin again.

Often people are reluctant to acknowledge the challenges they meet on the road to their dreams. There will always be distractions, detours, potholes and, sometimes, total derailments. Only by implementing skills that get you beyond these challenges can you move forward successfully. This manual encourages you to push on even when you feel you cannot go farther. Try your best to overcome the demons of inertia, procrastination, fear and lack of belief in self. Procrastination, especially, is the thief that steals your dreams. It hides in your habits.

Life is not just the good times. You live and breathe no matter how the winds of circumstance blow. Putting forth your best efforts only when life bends to your will, sets you up for heartache and frustration when you encounter bumps in the road. Challenge yourself with bold choices, decisions and actions, and the bumps become more manageable.

As is every person, you are endowed with a unique talent. It is not just about singing, dancing or superior athletic prowess. Talent is also the ability to develop an eye for color, see and sculpt images in a block of stone, tell a compelling story, love unconditionally, always see the best part of a person's nature, fuse diverse ingredients into a delicious meal, persevere relentlessly, speak the truth always, make logic from dissimilar patterns and see an opportunity when it presents itself, no matter how small. Your soul is unique in the universe, you belong here, or you would not have arrived. The joy in living your uniqueness is knowing you have a foundation on which to build your hopes and dreams. Remember, your talent is not an isolated corner of life. It is the wellspring from which your essence flows. It's that tiny seed that will eventually bear fruit in the garden of your dreams.

On the journey to goal you're competing with many previously learned habits and actions that you simply don't need any longer. But, you can be your strongest ally by developing appropriate skills. Your journey can be filled with joy, light, kindness, powerful words and determined actions, even when the wheels of life don't always turn smoothly. Your life has value, so the way you choose to live it cannot be by aimlessness or lawless dissipation, but with proven principles that always work.

To be truthful, you know the route to your goals and dreams because you have reached previously set goals. Hard work and sacrifice are major factors. So why do you sometimes hesitate? Fear may be the culprit. A vibrant life takes time, effort and perseverance. If longed-for goals don't materialize immediately or as soon as expected, you often quit. The effort may seem too great and you can't see the value in persevering. Your patience is in short supply. Once you allow this outlook to take hold, your goals and dreams become mere daydreams invoked to make you feel warm and take your mind off other problems.

That goal you expect to meet somewhere down the road has its roots in the choices and decisions you make today. Your decision to pursue a goal is the first step in your journey. The combination to unlock the door to your goal is simple. Take time to examine the goal. Determine its worth to you. Your mind takes control and ownership of those ideas you value. You hear self promises all the time. A friend will say, "I need to lose twenty-five pounds." "This year I'll get out of debt." "I'm going back to school and get my degree." "I'll beat this addiction." "This year I'm going back to church, finish my novel, no longer take this abuse from my spouse, boss or friend." "I'll find a more satisfying job . . . start my own business . . . save money to buy a home."

What promises did you make to yourself about change? The idea is to go beyond statements of intention and begin to construct a plan. In the twenty-first century, life is more complex than during the previous hundred years. This century demands competent decision making based on reliable information. It is, therefore, more difficult than ever to meet any goal without a solid plan and the courage to carry it to successful conclusion.

Define your goal and refine it as necessary. What need does the goal satisfy? It cannot be a vague idea of something you want to happen. Be specific. Be clear. Commit to it and stay focused. Concentrate and meditate. Question yourself. Are your current behaviors making a difference in your life? What is (or was) your best subject in school? Where have you excelled in your work? Are you a committee person or a solitary contributor? Are you eager to start early in the day or later? Do you understand how to make a plan? How can you include family and friends in this plan? Answers to these questions help identify and formulate your goal. You can taste and smell it. You're now hungry for its achievement.

With loving care use a few of your twenty-four hours each day getting to know yourself. Your vision will be clear of doubt and fear. Love of self demands respect and validity. Settle for no less. The value you place on yourself is the value the world accepts. That is the reason it is so important to have the true view of who you are and where you want to go in life. You're operating in truth when the foundation of your goal is anchored by your personal value system which in turn is bound to your life's purpose.

One note of caution, while working diligently toward your goal, fear of change will pay a visit or two. Just know change comes, either on tiny feet with sounds as soft as cotton or arrives like the sound of thunder. No matter how it enters your life, you can overcome fear or reduce any adverse effects of change with a solid plan and the boldness to act on it.

There may be other uninvited visitors: the shadow of doubt, negativity, a whisper of hopelessness or frustration during times when you find it difficult to go from point A to point B. Focus and refine your plan and you diminish the power of these villains. You will also come to a fork or two in the road. In choosing which direction to take, be authentic. The choice to make is the one that leads to your goal.

We start from different places in life. Maybe you knew early on which direction to take. It is likely you had nurturing parents, caring teachers, safe communities and hopeful people who walked through your life. They left you with the knowledge that possibilities are yours. You may have started later, encountering many barriers, but somehow believe you can backtrack and find the right road that leads to your dreams. On the other hand, if your dreams were stillborn, for you the journey will have extra challenges. No matter the point from which you began, the journey is yours alone. Every step brings you closer to your goal, even when walking through the lonely bumpy stretches with only your hopes for company.

If the road to your goal is wide, straight, level and smooth, this manual might serve as confirmation you're on the right path. The basis of any idea ultimately acted upon is the validity of information you possess at the time you make a decision. Without effective information you're acting blindly. Consider the manual a form of information gathering.

It's always beneficial to study the backgrounds of people who realized their goals and dreams. You'll see they did not just wander through their journeys. They set goals and saw possibilities beyond their current circumstances. Believing they could succeed they placed no limits on their imaginations and expectations. Gathering every resource available to them, including people, finances, skills, ideas and a way of thinking that allowed them to walk toward their dreams, became an integral part of their lives. Every aspect of existence had relevance even when they stumbled onto paths that weren't right before they found the one that supported their goals. These masters of goal achievement were always in learning mode, observing how decisions are made and incorporating new methods into their own plans. They never stopped trying to improve themselves.

Initially you're likely to have small successes which motivate and affirm your efforts. As you encounter and overcome new challenges brought about by change, you acquire additional skills. Your progress may plateau. But by staying focused and disciplined as you hone your skills; you continue moving forward with greater resolve. Constantly refresh these skills because they remain a necessary ingredient to your success. In the same way a house will collapse, if not maintained, so will your skills. A championship swimmer, who does not maintain her time by disciplined practice, loses her title. If potholes in streets are not repaired, they revert to ruts. Not practicing appropriate health habits, subjects you to disease. Organizing your affairs so that bills are paid on time is a financial skill. If not maintained, your credit worthiness is reduced. Three simple skills must be mastered if you're acquiring an education; attend classes (even if they're online), complete assignments and maintain an appropriate grade level. If you fail to preserve these skills as you go to higher levels, you eventually fall behind then dropped by the school.

There are no requirements for having a goal. You don't need a certification or college degree to dream, nor do you need someone else's approval. Don't wait for tomorrow, next week, next year, when you find the spouse of your dreams, when the children become independent and leave home, after receiving a loved one's consent, until you retire or some other time in the future to pursue your goals and dreams. Every day you hesitate is a choice that does not move you forward.

Of all the attributes you take on your journey, from the beginning integrity must be your constant companion. If not, your goal forever remains out of reach because when you act without integrity you're operating with an unstable foundation. Nothing you do can stand on that type of foundation.

The thrilling emotions you experience as you conquer the miles on the road to your dreams are so powerful there is little room for defeatism, hopelessness or feelings of victimization. You are taking responsibility for achievement of your goals.

Isn't that bountiful journey to goal worth another try? You bet it is. This little manual is meant as a reminder and encourager. As you study the skills suggested here, keep in mind it is written to give power to your struggles for goal fulfillment. These suggestions will fortify you for the potholes in the road ahead.

Make a Plan

Plan today for tomorrow
If not, for you, oh child of sorrow
For years to come, you're forced to borrow
Prepare today, my child, for tomorrow

I cannot overstate the importance of planning. A plan tells the story of your goal. Each step is a chapter filled with the drama of purpose, action and change. Developing a plan for goal achievement affirms your faith in the future. Your journey on the road to success begins with planning. Think forward. A well-prepared plan lights the way to your goal, step by step. It fosters development of necessary skills and habits. Your plan must be tight, legal, ethical and comport with your belief system and societal standards. Lax planning gives you an out when times get tough. With a plan you eliminate guessing and confusion. First be clear about the reasons you adopted the goal. Only the use of clear language supports goal achievement. If you are ambivalent about your motives, you'll not be motivated to persevere through the challenges.

Detailed planning will help you recognize where research and additional information are needed.

Planning is a problem solving process that assists in working through the issues and challenges you'll certainly encounter during your journey. Every part of the plan should move you closer to your goal. You don't need a complex scheme. Keep the plan simple. A simple plan organizes your thoughts and directs your actions. Be authentic. Monitor the narrative you use to move your goals forward. Screen out negative drumbeats that say you can't. Be bold and filled with expectation for a positive outcome. Believe in your plan and your actions will reflect that belief with competent and efficient behavior. Prepare the plan as you would any endeavor by making sure the process is moving you toward goal.

> Your dream is hope looking for a plan

Make your plan flexible, because as you execute each step you're poised to see additional opportunities or you may discover an unnecessary step that can be omitted. Your plan can't exist only in your head. Write it out and you can refer to it anytime. Initially write down every step, without thinking about what might be "stupid" or "wasted." A written plan reveals patterns that help and patterns that are barriers to forward movement. By clearly defining your goal you're in a position to choose and include only those steps necessary for its achievement.

Think of your plan as a road map that takes you from starting point to destination. Imagine, you decide to drive from West Virginia to Oregon. You get on the nearest interstate, not knowing whether it runs east to west or north to south. You have a fifty/fifty chance of reaching your destination, meaning you may never reach Oregon.

Without a plan, success of your goal

> You are the architect of your plan, design it well

is elusive and will forever remain beyond your grasp. If you're not sure how to begin a plan, start by reviewing your life and noting the times you were successful in your endeavors. Record your behavior and the habits leading to your successes. Then separately, record the times you did not obtain the goals you set. I'm willing to posit, the successes followed a plan. Your plan is the foundation for goal achievement.

A valid plan is grounded by credible assumptions. These assumptions act like the brick and concrete blocks that form the foundation of a building. Weak assumptions cannot support your efforts for goal fulfillment. The assumptions you rely on when making a plan are effective to the outcome of your efforts only if they are undergirded with facts. A basic assumption includes the belief you're moving in the right direction toward your goal, only if the goal is infused with your life's purpose and value system. Assume you've considered all possibilities for success, have necessary facts and meaningful information for making a plan that is achievable.

Be as detailed as you can at the initial planning stage

The more detailed you are in planning, the fewer surprises you encounter during your journey. Include every step you

> Your purpose is the muscle that lifts your plan

can identify, at this point. Your education, experience, recreational pursuits and life's work help form the necessary steps. As you execute the plan each step is a guide.

At the planning stage, cost is a necessary consideration, but should not be the only consideration. If you fall into that trap, you then place limits on your success by allowing cost to stand as a sentinel blocking the door to your dreams. If you're planning to buy a stroller for your child, grandchild, niece, nephew or as a gift, you want the best stroller for the least cost. You wouldn't buy the cheapest stroller just because it's cheap. Your purchase must balance safety with cost.

All ideas that you consider during the planning stage have value. How you connect and implement them will depend on your resources, time constraints and nature of your goal. Many of these ideas are needed at different stages of your journey. It's best to include them in your possibilities. In time, as you monitor your progress, you'll find the right place for them and understand how to combine these ideas for the greatest effort. Further, many of these initial ideas help in mining for new methods.

Don't include anything that doesn't allow you to rethink or alter one of the steps you initially included. An example is the goal to save monthly for a down payment of $10,000.00 on the purchase of a house. Save $300.00 each

> Consider cost and value—they make a strong team

month for six months. Then begin saving $350.00 per month for six months. Finally increase your savings to $400.00 per month. Have this sum automatically deducted from your checking account and placed in a separate savings account specifically for the down payment. Eventually, you accumulate the sum needed. Suppose, however, after saving for twelve months, you have an emergency—car needs a major repair. Reduce your automatic savings by $200.00 until you solve the car emergency, and then return to the dedicated savings sum. Success is aided by your ability to monitor and make adjustments when required.

As you develop your plan, recognize supporting skills such as prioritizing steps, securing additional information, paying attention to details, honing interpersonal skills and disciplining your actions. Be careful this process does not become so all-encompassing that planning itself becomes the de facto goal. That is procrastination, not planning. Even if your plan mandates a change because of an unexpected emergency, never lose focus on the goal.

To that end, an important skill is learning how to get beyond obstacles you may not have identified or could not anticipate at the beginning of your journey, such as the unexpected car repair.

You may find it necessary to gather around you a solid team. Members of this group may be so identified during the initial planning. If you discover others who can add value to your efforts, include them. There may be inspiring and motivating people outside your team with skills you can emulate. But they must be people you respect and trust to be honest, truthful and reliable. Accordingly, your plan should include specific support you expect from them. This expectation, however, does not relieve you of personal responsibility for the plan's implementation. Your knowledge of the nuts and bolts of your goal is essential in getting the best assistance from the team. It is helpful to have a diverse group of people by age, experience in the area of your goal and someone with the confidence to disagree with you when necessary.

> The seed you sow
> is the plant you get

Consider a mentor. If you do, make sure you know why you need one. Is it to counsel in an area you need expertise? Can this person link you to people at the next level who are able to point out bumps and potholes you need to anticipate and overcome? Will the mentor advise what is expected of you at the present or as a foundation for the future? Be clear so the benefits of this resource are not squandered.

Truth and clarity work together in your plan. Like strands in a net, they strengthen each other. You'll never have clarity if your actions are based on lies. Whether what you are seeing and hearing is clear, factual and logical will determine the information's truthfulness. Your decisions at this stage should augment the plan, not undermine it. Therefore, base your decisions on facts as they are, not as you wish them to be. Likewise, as you assess and make decisions about people, your trust must be based on the factual evidence of their character, not on an idealized vision of how you think those people should be or act.

> Goal achievement rises and thrives in truth

You are familiar with two stunning historical failures because of planning errors, Napoleon in 1812 and the German army during World War II. A major reason they lost their battles to defeat Russia was because of failure to include clarity about the severity of Russian winters. Both of these armies failed in planning to properly equip their soldiers for combat during the brutal Russian winter months. On the other hand, every one of you reading this manual has experienced at least one excellent example of planning that resulted in success: your ability to read. The teachers who taught you to read began with lesson plans that moved you step by step, from word sounds to vocabulary to sentence structure and finally comprehension, culminating in your ability to recognize, comprehend and use words.

First things first. You hear that phrase all the time, but what does it really mean? In preparing and executing a plan there is a necessary act which must be completed before you can successfully move to the next step. If left uncompleted or not given the attention required, you waste valuable time and possibly miss opportunities because there is a link to the next level, which is missing. Each part of your plan, therefore, must proceed in a logical march to completion. With a sound plan, you always know where you are and alerted immediately if you're off-course.

> Imagine beyond
> your fears

The plan may require additional information readily available in local libraries, specialized collections, archives and of course the Internet. Additional sources of valuable information are also held in family histories, institutional memory and by local legends in your community who inspired others to dream big when setting goals. In my own community there was a man who, with little resources, began publishing a small weekly newspaper. This publisher had an idea that people wanted to read news about themselves that was not being reported in the major daily papers. His goal was to publish stories about local events, community leaders, strategies to help the community move forward, school issues and historical milestones. He made a plan that included getting subscribers, finding stories, hiring employees and obtaining equipment and supplies. The paper sold at an affordable price. After more than half a century The Miami Times continues to report on community events, people of note and other important issues. There are subscribers all over the globe.

> Time is a gift; respect its limitations and opportunities

While planning, you need to connect the points of your life by incorporating the processes that led to goal achievement in the past. You are the sum of your past, present, family customs, gender, ethnicity and culture. Every aspect of your being comes to the planning process. There you find lessons, directions and valuable experiences on which you can rely for support.

Plan for the unexpected by knowing changes will occur that may require alterations in the plan. If you have not navigated a pothole, rest assured before you arrive at your goal, you will confront one or more of these challenges and be called upon to act in circumstances outside your plan. Understand the challenges and competing risks. Quickly identify what must be done, access assistance needed, act boldly and internalize the lessons.

Developing appropriate skills is the only route to your goal. Without them you spin your wheels, resulting in no movement forward. Different levels in your plan may require additional skills. At the very beginning assess the skills you already possess. This process also identifies other skills needed. Make no doubt about it; you have certain basic skills that are transferable to any situation. Look at the skills you use as you move through your day—prioritizing projects, focusing on one thing at a time, knowing when to take a break, organizing your thoughts and practicing timeliness. All your

> Truth, gives power to purpose, plans and actions

skills become stronger when you combine new skills with existing skills. Further, you begin to recognize which skills are interchangeable. These crossover skills are the most valuable because neural connections produced in the brain expand their capabilities. They help establish, maintain and strengthen habits. Likewise, habits develop and strengthen skills. They work together.

Many recent historical events started with a plan and progressed to successful conclusions following the same universal principles, skills and actions I suggest in this little manual. During the last century women were given voting rights. Social Security benefits were established to provide more comfortable retirement years for seniors. African Americans obtained civil rights in education, public accommodations, housing, voting and employment. These monumental movements began with a goal to establish equality for all Americans. I encourage you to examine important events in your life and you'll note each one involved commitment to the execution of a plan.

The quality of my own life was elevated by a plan during the civil rights struggles. During my last year at Talladega College the student body association made a decision **(goal)** to march for equal rights to public accommodations. We developed a **(plan)** for a protest march in Anniston, Alabama, approximately twenty miles from campus. The association held several meetings in

> Embrace truth,
> it liberates

the student center to map out **(steps)** for executing this plan: electing team leaders, selecting a date, transportation method, number of participants, gathering information about possible barriers to the march, challenges during the march such as safety concerns and fears of parents and the type of training we needed in the dynamics of non-violent protest. Our **(commitment)** was strengthened as we gathered additional information and discussed risks. The daily meetings, pep rallies and dissemination of new information kept our **(focus)** on the upcoming march. The students consistently reviewed the information obtained, our strategy and anticipated challenges **(discipline)**. We continued our efforts, answering questions about risks and, of course parental concerns. Not once did we discuss cancelling our plans **(perseverance)**. On the day of the march our determined attitude accompanied us to Anniston where we walked amid frightening jeers and threats. Upon our return to the campus, we reviewed the event and our participation in the beginning of a momentous time in history. We were successful in the mission to do our part in breaking down the walls of segregation because we prepared a plan and persevered to its conclusion.

Remember, a dream is hope looking for a plan. On the road to your goal, hope cannot stand alone. An attitude buttressed by hope can move your thinking forward, however relying only on hope, leaves you at your starting point, merely nurturing a daydream. Planning provides structure and a logical path to follow.

Specific recommendations for planning

1. **Understand the planning process before you begin to make a plan.** Research this process if planning is new to you. The plan is a sequenced guide and as with any guide, it exists to move you on the journey to your goal. As you begin the planning process, you will not have all the answers to your questions and concerns. But you do have information available at your fingertips.

2. **Recognize a solid plan reduces uncertainty and enhances predictability for the success of your plan.** The unexpected events that arise will be less scary. The plan boosts your efforts to keep moving by leading you logically from step to step. It is easy to be seduced by distractions. For that reason your plan should not be complex. When you adopt a complex plan, you're more susceptible to distractions.

3. **Construct the plan so your goal always remains in sight.** Planning step by step you

avoid inadvertently erecting barriers because the plan represents your vision for a specific outcome. A solid plan assists in identifying ambiguities, falsehoods and confusion. The minute a step becomes complicated or ambiguous, question whether it leads to your goal. You get your answer by breaking that step into smaller parts and examining each one for authenticity.

4. **Nurture a clear vision of your goal.** Reduce your plan to a written document. If the plan exists only in your head or on scattered pieces of paper, you lose by not having a document to which you can easily refer or alter as needed. People who realized their dreams and goals were able to visualize them every step of their journeys. Study their lives. Examine the strategies they used in keeping clear sight of their goals. Pay particular attention to those who achieved their goals in the area you are pursuing.

5. **Study how others have overcome obstacles and barriers on the road to their goals.** Research of their biographical sketches helps. Through this process you're in a position to adopt proven strategies that alert you to obstacles ahead and how to move around them.

6. **Understand that even though your plan is a dynamic guide, it should be flexible enough to allow for alternatives and changes when necessary.** You can be sure as you move forward change will alter parts of the plan;

therefore the plan must allow you space to incorporate unexpected and unfamiliar circumstances.

7. **Acquire and assess knowledge about the specific goal for which you are planning.** Include as much about your goal as you have identified at the initial planning stage. You must acquire deep knowledge of the details of your goal. Evaluate the knowledge you have and research additional knowledge needed. It is vital that you understand the nuts and bolts of achieving the goal. Pay particular attention to details such as any certification or license required.

8. **Know the questions to ask.** Don't ask questions that give only the answers you want. Ask questions that give truth. Relying on false information impairs your efforts. Questions should produce answers based in fact not emotions. If the answers to your questions do not settle the issues, you have asked the wrong questions.

9. **Identify tools needed to reach your goal.** As much as you are able at the starting point, identify time frame, people, expenses and possible professional talent needed for achievement. You are adding value to future efforts.

10. **Anticipate roadblocks and potholes you expect to encounter during the journey to goal.** You are able to anticipate many time issues and challenges if there are large blocks

of time devoted to employment, family, social obligations or other commitments previously made. Anticipate any objections to your goal by people in your life whose opinions are important to you. A major consequence of goal pursuit is change. There are people you trust who become uncomfortable with the changes they see in you and not accept them. However, as your focus naturally becomes more centered on the steps to goal achievement there may be a reduction in the time previously given to these important people in your life. This change tends to frighten them. They may erect roadblocks. Be prepared to resist the barriers they present by not honoring them.

11. **Estimate the monetary costs required to achieve your goal.** It is essential you are honest when anticipating any financial issues you may encounter. An informed estimate at the beginning prevents waste of financial resources. It also provides a baseline to rein in costs. Know your financial position. If your goal requires money and you lack clarity about your finances, but proceed with this faulty information, from the start your plan stands on shaky ground because you're not operating in truth.

12. **Organize the plan so you are more efficient in your movement forward.** You're developing the skill of prioritizing your efforts. Include provisions specifically dedicated

to alternatives. In time you'll acquire the information to choose between competing options. Suppose you have a goal to remodel your kitchen. Your plan includes a cost estimate that reflects your budget. Your first option is to enlarge the room by removing a wall. You've made an alternate plan that does not include the wall removal. Your contractor determines a support beam has to be installed if you remove the wall. This increases costs beyond the budget. Because you have two options you can still remodel the kitchen within your budget using the second option. Another example is an invitation to a friend for an event you plan to host, which includes an alternate rain date.

13. **Review and monitor progress toward your goal.** This skill is necessary as a check on the continued validity of the steps in your plan. If you stray off course, you can quickly identify any errors and move to correct them.

14. **Know when to add previously unidentified steps or subtract unnecessary steps in the plan.** Acquisition of additional information may necessitate a step that could not be anticipated during the planning stage. Likewise, you are able to alter or eliminate steps that no longer move you forward. Example. Your goal is to reduce your cholesterol number. Your first step is to change eating habits by eating more leafy green vegetables and fewer desserts. You include an increased level of exercise and

the purchase of new exercise gear. Good plan. Further on, your numbers are not going down. Your physician advises the addition of medication—a step you had not included, but now can consider. You also find there is no need to buy special clothes for exercise. There are shorts, pants and tops in your closet. This is a step you can eliminate.

15. **Develop the ability to set a time frame for achievement of your goal.** When you don't set time limits, you're giving yourself permission to waste time. Time limits keep you moving. Set smaller goals to be achieved at specified intervals; daily, weekly or monthly. You become more focused. Remember you are competing with old habits. This skill puts you on the winning side.

16. **Understand you take every aspect of yourself on your journey.** The five-year-old child you once were, the high school student, that person starting her first job, biases, cultural references and habits, the feelings that swept over you when you experienced a special joy, the hurt when someone you loved let you down—all of these issues will accompany you. It is, therefore, important when you prepare your plan to expect them in the backpack you carry. Some of these experiences will escape the backpack and trip you or quietly suggest you turn right when you should turn left. Their weight may become so heavy; they begin to act like saboteurs. But whatever they are, be

assured, goal achievement is impacted by them. Initially identify patterns that concern you and continually show up in your life such as the habit of procrastination or proceeding with a project without sufficient knowledge or information. Ignoring these patterns will delay or abort your goal achievement.

17. **Develop your plan in a manner that permits collaborative efforts.** You may need to connect with another person, group or institution in solving issues that arise during the planning process and beyond. It is unlikely you can achieve your goal standing alone. Collaboration provides you with additional information, resources, support and opportunities. Therefore, be open to these options especially in areas outside your strengths. As a caution, do not make any part of your plan contingent on sabotaging someone else's journey.

18. **Anticipate consequences as you develop your plan.** What are the likely results of actions you take with the steps in your plan, especially consequences related to procrastination? Consider some of the consequences of wrong habits: undisciplined behaviors, negative thoughts and efforts, diminished sense of possibilities, using excuses and blaming others. At this planning stage if you recognize any of these behaviors in yourself, know they affect your goal achievement. Deal with them in truth if positive change is to occur.

Commit to Your Plan

Commit your all
Each resource standing tall
To avoid a future fall,
So listen child, don't drop the ball

Commitment validates your trust in the planning process. It is the broadest of the five keys to goal achievement I suggest in this manual. It is here you begin the process of attitude adjustment and change in habits. You confront your identity, experience and history. This attribute begins even before planning starts. The unconditional passion for and belief in your goal is the core of all your efforts. Commitment keeps the many moving parts of your goal oiled and working together. It will sustain your momentum and reenergize your efforts when movement forward begins to slow. When you commit to a plan you are personally responsible for its implementation and outcome, giving the plan priority placement on your to-do list. Your commitment must be total. If you are half-hearted in committing yourself to this plan, which represents your life's purpose, no one else will come on board with you. Family or friends may commit for a while, but even their zeal, unshared by your efforts, will slow and eventually stop.

Attitude

Attitude is the result of your belief system, choices, worldview, conditioning, thought processes and your responses to outside

> Challenges will find you, don't look for them

stimuli. How you learned to interpret and internalize events in your environment will affect your attitude and behavior. Commitment is a purpose-driven attitude representing your belief that the goal is attainable.

Manage your thinking by training yourself to filter out negative slants. Turn them around to the positive. If you begin to see a negative point of view first, reject it, again and again if necessary, until it no longer has a place in your mind. You then begin to develop an attitude that the only direction is forward, toward your goal.

As you seek information and pose questions, phrase queries that give useful answers. Suppose you're nurturing the goal of purchasing a house and need information about costs. You ask, "Will I ever be able to save enough to buy a house?" How is this question different from, "How much money do I need to save to buy a house? How much money can I save this year? How much can I save each pay period?" With the first question you start from a weak position. You are questioning your ability to own a home. This allows weakness to stand as a barrier to your commitment. The next series of questions contain built-in assumptions that you are capable and they lead to answers of specific amounts you need to save for the purchase of a house. They're even posed in the nature of a plan with steps: total costs, amount you can amass in a year and the amount you need to save each pay period. Answers to these questions force action if your goal is authentic.

You have choices, don't waste these opportunities

If you are committed to your goal, you do not place conditions on your time, but use every available hour to reach the goal. You begin to think, "I will use the time I have" and let go of the attitude, "I will find time somehow." You don't have to look for time. It's not lost. Time exists automatically, just waiting for you to engage its unlimited possibilities. Every person on the planet has twenty-four hours each day and three hundred sixty-five days (three sixty-six every four years), in a year. How successful you are in achieving the goals you set is determined by your use of these hours and days. Time is a commodity owned by everyone. It has no allegiance to any particular person. Your neighbor, competitor or colleague owns no more hours in a day than you. Time rewards the person who understands its possibilities and respects its limitations. You've heard the adage, "Use your time wisely." Time has many components; minutes, hours, days, weeks, months, years and beyond. Consistently using even one of them adds power to each step of your journey. Poor use of time leaves your dreams unrealized. The only choice is to make time an ally.

Avoid toxic emotions such as envy, vengeance, greed or sense of slight. When they come upon you, examine and counter them. Disable envious emotions by knowing that those you envy are where they are because of their own choices and actions. What you see are the fruits of their goals and dreams. Vengeful thoughts consume energy that is better used to fuel your own dreams. Vengeance is often confused with justice; therefore its effect on you is powerful. Every time you think vengeance, tell yourself to put this energy into your plan. That sense of slight you may feel is really a diminishing of your own self worth and value. You are surrendering power over your emotions to someone else. Your feelings of slight indicate a perception that you are entitled to another's attention.

> Decisions determine actions and consequences

Use empowering language

Learn to harness the force of language in fashioning the road to your dreams. As you formulate your plan speak to your hopes and dreams. Literally, encourage yourself by speaking aloud. It helps.

Using encouraging language to support goal achievement connects your desire to behavior that supports your efforts. Words such as opportunity, responsibility, empowerment, knowledge and hope expand your vision of possibilities and options and link you to unforeseen opportunities. When you follow the trail of these new options and possibilities, your

> Your future resides in your actions today

focus eliminates falsehoods, misunderstandings and wrong conclusions. These words of power bring clarity and truth to the achievement process. They reinforce new habits and strengthen your expanded mindset. By using words that enable you to move with confidence toward your goals, you're liberated from mental roadblocks holding you in place. Likewise, negative words have the power to erect barriers that slow progress or derail your efforts.

Successes may depend on particular terms you use to describe the plan. Use the language of your goal. If your goal is education there is a specific structure for word usage when communicating in the academic world. The same stands for the fields of law, medicine, human resources, finance, entrepreneurship, mathematics and engineering. If you're deciding to repair and refresh your financial foundation, how do you describe your efforts? Are you relying on a budget or creating a new money management plan? The word budget sounds limiting. Immediately it produces fear and feelings of uncertainty. A money management plan, on the other hand, is expansive and allows you the freedom to see possibilities, not limits. Using the term, "crash diet" as opposed to "revised eating plan" has a different connotation if you're working on weight reduction. The former sets up barriers to what you can eat. The latter expands your options. Appropriate language sends the message you want directly to your brain.

> Optimism is infectious, spread it around

Use it to your advantage every step of your journey. Free yourself from the tyranny of phrases such as; It's too late. I'm too old. What's the point? I'm jinxed. This is too hard. My family always lived this way. These statements are self-imposed barriers to opportunities that flow naturally from positive language. Instead, substitute; I can do this, I'll start now, I need to change my outlook and any other positive affirmation.

Some familiar language might include:

- "I've been good this week, so I can eat a couple of doughnuts."
- "This blouse is just what I'm looking for. I can charge the $85.00."
- "I won't put any money in my savings account this month, I'll double the amount next month."

This type of internal narrative leads to faulty reasoning that delays or derails goal achievement.

The power of language will even persuade you to other actions, which move you backward instead of in the direction of goal achievement. You are constantly bombarded with powerful language. It is therefore, important you learn to distinguish messages delivered through symbols and

> You waste valuable time making choices for others

coded speech from information containing facts that lead to successes. Consider words used by sellers and marketers that persuade you to purchase items you can't afford or need. Marketing language is aimed at your decision making process. The purpose of this type of word usage is to eliminate time you deliberate between hearing the language and making a decision, thereby urging you to accept the marketer's choice. Market your own plan to yourself by the language you allow into your head.

Personal responsibility is paramount

Taking personal responsibility is the first step to goal achievement. Move your life forward toward your goals with the choices and decisions you make. The integrity of your decisions is based on the quality of information you consider. Gathering facts is easier today than for previous generations. Information is no farther than your keyboard. Technology allows access to needed information through computers, cell phones and other personal electronic devices. Always be conscious of your choices and decisions so you don't fall into the trap of blaming others when you meet hard times or encounter circumstances that slow your progress. The choice you make today is the law you live with tomorrow.

Be tenacious in pulling all your resources together

> One change today, forever changes tomorrow

for the ultimate purpose of goal fulfillment. Never lament what you don't have. By relying on resources available to you, without wasting energy wishing for more, you use these resources more efficiently. They begin to perform more than one function. Your ability to see additional uses for each resource is enhanced.

Once you take personal responsibility for yourself, you graduate from school, save and accumulate funds to purchase a home, take care of your health, manage resources, save for retirement and always monitor your progress. In accepting personal responsibility for goal achievement, you don't envy others. Instead you see another person's success as a motivating force. The habit of taking responsibility enforces self-motivation and adds to the foundation of success, which builds on itself. You're more open to new ideas and changes. You act boldly, avoiding a wait-and-see attitude, which is nothing more than procrastination.

When you take responsibility for your goals and dreams, you let go of any attitude of entitlement. You are only entitled to free will and choice. Once you begin to feel you're entitled to particular circumstances, it becomes easy to shift responsibility to others for completion of your goals. Shedding your own responsibility prevents forward movement. You squander energy pursuing entitlements instead of skills necessary to make competent decisions.

> Authenticity never lies

Ownership

You are more disciplined when you own your goals and plan for their fulfillment. With the attribute of ownership, the balance of power is weighted on your side. You get up early and stay up late to remain focused on your goals and to persevere when times get tough. When you take ownership of your goals you treat them with the loving care befitting their importance.

Ownership empowers. When you own your goals and dreams, their fulfillment requires ownership of your thoughts and actions. You'll have trouble moving forward if you surrender control of your goals and dreams to someone else's actions. If you do, that person may lack the necessary enthusiasm, passion and crucial knowledge. Achieving your goals may be slowed or halted. Without ownership, you miss the important elements of focus and commitment and the opportunity to acquire new skills for achievement. Your ability to anticipate challenges diminishes. The efficient use of time is lost to your control. Your dream is at risk of fading into the realm of wishful thinking. The assumptions of that other person for success may not be your assumptions.

> Remember your history, it's ripe with lessons

Be prepared for opportunities when they appear

Being ready for opportunities means you are resourceful, open to change and calculated risk taking. You weigh your options and opportunities against the fear of taking action, and then decide which will lead to your goal. Calculated risk taking involves the introduction of new people and circumstances into your life. The formation of a new set of dynamics might set the stage for conflicts. With clearly defined goals and positive habits you're encouraged to act appropriately in resolving these conflicts, by developing an attitude open to compromise. As you assess these opportunities also trust your instincts for their validity.

Learn to listen. This is another method of obtaining information that may lead to new opportunities. Don't try to guess what is being said. You miss good information. Listen carefully to the point the speaker emphasizes and the extras you may not have expected. Often when you say you're listening to the other person in a conversation, what you are really doing is waiting anxiously to say your piece. You're only listening for a break in the conversation to begin speaking again. So much is missed. However, if you genuinely participate in a conversation by hearing the other party, you are able to respond appropriately and get additional information. By listening, you're

> Don't let issues from your past hijack your future

also developing a strong people-skill demonstrating to the speaker you care about what she's saying. This opens further opportunities from the speaker that may link you to greater possibilities.

Know yourself

Knowing yourself is an important skill you cannot overlook in pursuit of your goals and dreams. As you move through your plan, you'll learn more about yourself and the frame of reference from which you view the world. Becoming more aware of the dynamics of your personal history, you encounter less confusion and ambiguity on the journey to goal. A clearer vision of the requirements for goal achievement emerges. Divide your life into segments and study each period. Recognize patterns of behavior emerging that support your goals or those that are likely to sabotage them. Note the patterns that moved you forward. They will work again. As an example, look at your childhood. Your role probably consisted of obeying parents' house rules and going to school. During that time you learned the importance of respecting boundaries and basic societal rules. There was predictable structure in your life. Structure promotes discipline, which is a cornerstone of goal achievement. This personal examination is also important in recognizing your strengths.

> Never be a puppet, dance to your own music

You are the sum of what you think, how you think, the forces you expose yourself to, people you expose yourself to, the words you use and decisions you make. Also, your age, marriage status, number of people you're responsible for, whether you are still in the education process, expenses you must meet and other obligations are significant factors in goal achievement.

Individual situations, events and circumstances in your life hold other valuable lessons for goal fulfillment. Examine carefully your motive for pursuing specific outcomes. Is the goal for your satisfaction or is it someone else's unfulfilled dream? Remember, another person's dream rises from a different life experience. This honest view of yourself helps identify barriers to even more positive actions. Only if you are concrete in assessing a goal will you have clarity that the goal aligns with your purpose. Consider this example. You're a math whiz. Your power with numbers was recognized by your kindergarten teacher. Moving through school the ability to add multiple columns of numbers, your mastery of numerical patterns, confidence to perform "number tricks" at parties, successfully completing advanced math placement courses, you claimed every math prize. After graduating from college, you decided to share your joy of numbers and become a high school math teacher. Family and friends, however, convinced you to use your natural talent in a different profession, one paying six-figures. After five years your lack of enthusiasm begins to drain energy from daily activities and your job performance suffers. For two more years you forge on. Finally, you ask yourself, "Am I living my life at cross purposes?" A yes answer requires reassessment of your professional goal by answers to additional questions. Are you living in the truth of your unique math talent? Does your present job align with your purpose to teach young people? Does the six-figure salary bring joy into your life? Are you working at your highest level? If you answer no to these questions, then the present job is a barrier to your original goal of becoming a high school math teacher. Your choice to take the higher salary is not aligned with your natural talent. Review the plan you made for your professional life and rearrange the steps.

> You can never justify injustice, you always lose

While looking into the corners of your life, don't ignore the dark corners you find. Those dusty ghosts still have the power to stall your dreams. They emerge in your fears and doubts. Can you see situations or patterns when you wanted to manifest a specific outcome, but gave up even before you began your pursuit? Scrutinize the circumstances and your emotions surrounding these instances. What initiated your hesitation to act? What else was occurring in your life during these periods? Answer these questions

> Hope has legs, keep them moving

as best you can. Once you are able to identify the markers you can rob them of power with information and skills suggested in this manual.

In the game of life, you are your fiercest competitor. Therefore, you can only compete effectively if you're free of fear, anger, envy, hatred and negative thoughts. By committing to your goal achievement, you recognize the destructive force of these demons. Confront them, tear them apart, study them and the reasons they're in your life. Choose to rid yourself of these unproductive emotions. They then begin to shrink as barriers to your dreams.

Every person has a dream for her life, in that most secret of secret places. The dream blooms and dances in color. It cannot be denied, notwithstanding, there are those who are content to daydream rather than make their dreams come to fruition. You know your dreams better than anyone. You can see them, smell them, and even taste their special flavors. So why not act on them? Fear is usually the culprit. It stalks your world like a voracious monster paralyzing your actions. Know the fears and why you're afraid to act. Ask yourself questions that unlock the door of these fears. Are you afraid because you fear losing control if you make changes or do you fear unfamiliar situations and circumstances? For additional help in conquering these fears, start small by seeking information or consulting a professional who can help answer your

> Commitment is the backbone of change

questions. Then move beyond your fears to the next step in the plan and act on it.

Recalling instances when you made a goal come true, how much time did you commit? What resources were necessary? How did you feel? Name that part of your inner self that kept your commitment intact. Those strategies and lessons will work again. Remember as a child, when you wanted a special toy from your parents; you came up with a plan. You promised to be "good" or "do extra chores." Your plan to get a new toy was simple. Simplicity still works. It's a bulwark against ambiguity.

As your commitment becomes stronger, you encounter situations that require negotiation. Be flexible. Negotiation has the power to expand opportunities by introducing alternatives. If circumstances cause a stumble, get up, assess the reasons, make appropriate adjustments and move forward.

Anticipate stress

Be prepared for stress when you are at work on your plan and life interferes with a must-do project or another emergency. If the project has a legitimately higher priority, then complete it or it might become a distraction. Heightened stress often produces physical symptoms. Recognize your own symptoms. For me when I am under a heightened level of stress, the stress short-circuits my memory. I must then stop and calm myself before moving forward. If you experience this type of lapse, no matter how brief, it is likely to interfere with the pursuit of your goals. Take the time needed to lower your stress level. Don't sink into a funk. Keep moving. It's important that you learn to live in that stressful place between the highs and lows. It can be a lonely and dangerous place, but it is in that stretch of your journey that all your hopes, dreams and efforts must be preserved.

It's easy to become self-absorbed during these times. You may not want to take phone calls or interact with family, friends or co-workers. Your only desire is to focus on working toward your goal. Balance these competing necessities and you'll feel more fulfilled as you move forward.

All of your previous experiences have produced skills for living, surviving and prospering. Even the stressful experiences you did not want or expect have value. From those you learned life lessons that foster strong commitment. You learned what works and what should be avoided in future endeavors.

Specific behaviors that strengthen your commitment efforts

1. **Learn to gather and interpret additional information.** Only by relying on relevant information will you have credible outcomes. As your skill level increases, you recognize the need for additional information. Your interpretation of this information affects your ability to make effective decisions. It is imperative the interpretation stands up to the truth of your purpose in pursuing the goal.

2. **Use skills acquired through your distinct cultural affiliation.** Certain customs and life skills imbedded in your culture will assist you during the journey. They are valuable assets. If you don't use these skills, you miss the potential they offer. Assess and sift through all of these skills, not only the ones you think will help you reach goal, but also those that hold the possibility of additional opportunities. The prism through which you view expectations, interpret facts, your attitude of accepting new ideas, work ethic and changes in circumstances have cultural references. It is, therefore, important to examine and correctly interpret these references in light of your goals. Culture is powerful. It has the capacity to override education and training. Look out for those aspects of your culture that do not move you forward. Always be sure the

movement forward aligns with your personal principles, which are largely set by cultural cues. If your culture promotes risk taking, for example, you will have less fear of the risks involved in setting and achieving goals, especially if your goal is to start a new business, relocate for greater professional opportunities or pursue a non-traditional career path. The value your culture places on self-reliance boosts your discipline and perseverance skills. If education has a high premium in your culture, it will be reflected in your commitment to learning new skills. This means you begin the journey with one of the most powerful resources required for success, relevant cultural assets.

3. **See opportunity in every circumstance.** Each skill you acquire widens your opportunity base. The strength of your efforts depends on adopting and using additional skills at the new levels.

4. **Continue to monitor your plan and progress.** As you add and strengthen the skills necessary to move forward to your goal, it's a good idea to revisit the plan and possibly reprioritize, rearrange or alter certain steps.

5. **Develop the ability to make correct choices by considering all information available to you:** information from previous experiences, new information, current circumstances, any cultural affiliation and sources of assistance.

Examine this information and choose those aspects that lead to success. This can only be done if you understand and interpret facts correctly.

6. **Learn to make the choice that leads to your desired outcome.** Keep in mind different choices require the input of different information. You will be making choices every step of your journey. In the same way a muscle responds to exercise, by getting stronger, increasing use of this skill, lessens your fear of decision making.

7. **Develop the ability, when making decisions, to look beyond current circumstances to consequences.** This skill assists in avoiding mistakes that may result from faulty thinking or unreliable information.

8. **Develop the ability to remain focused.** Only by maintaining a 20/20 view of your goal will you be able to avoid unnecessary actions, which waste time and energy.

9. **Learn to think in a manner that empowers your efforts.** Get rid of fear with appropriate information, then act boldly and trust yourself.

10. **Learn to eliminate negative thought patterns, unproductive behaviors and outdated actions by reframing them.** They are toxic to your emotions and affect your actions. Break the link by learning to deflect negative self-talk. Reverse and reframe limiting narratives:

- "I can't," becomes "I will gather information so that I can," or "There is a way I can do this."
- "This is so hard. I'll never be able to finish on time," becomes "This weekend I'll sacrifice my Saturday outing so I can finish on schedule."
- "My son can't go to science camp in July because I don't have enough money," becomes "I have four months to save for camp fees. I can save $75.00 every two weeks."

The simplest way to understand reframing is by using the example of a picture hanging in your family room with a frame that no longer works with the room's décor. You decide the picture is still beautiful, but the frame has to go. The new frame is a better complement to the room's current style. So it is on the road to your goals and dreams. If you have surrounded an essential belief with a frame that does not promote your movement forward, reframe. Reframing requires extraordinary effort because you are supplanting an established belief which goes to the heart of your personal identity. By challenging this belief you challenge your self perception. On the road to goal fulfillment there may come a time when reframing must take place. The frame around an old belief must be removed and a new frame installed. Suppose your (**goal**) is to buy a home. You believe the purchase can be financed with little or no money down, similar to making a credit card purchase (**old frame surrounding your goal**). Today banks require a substantial down payment. Your goal is still authentic; however you need to accumulate an acceptable sum. After acquiring additional information you still believe you can purchase a house by saving enough to satisfy a lender (**new frame**). Reframing is a skill that will work in all aspects of your life. Another example: You want your preteen daughter to keep her room clean (**goal**). Because she doesn't comply, you become annoyed and place her in time-out again and again (**old frame surrounding goal**). The power struggle between you and your daughter continues. Clothes are on the floor, bed is unmade, school books and papers are all over the room in disarray. The room needs to be cleaned and she's old enough to do it. The goal is still appropriate, but it's time to reframe your belief that time-outs will encourage her to clean the room. Try withholding your consent if she wants to go swimming, skating, spend time with friends or some other pleasure she desires (**new frame**).

11. **Learn to compete with yourself.** As your most formidable competitor you're battling personal unworkable attitudes and habits.

With self-motivated competition you win by attacking your own weaknesses. The battle can only be fought and won with appropriate skills which neutralize your fears, freeing more energy for goal achievement.

12. **Develop resilience by first accepting change will occur in your life and affect the attainment of your goals.** By refusing to allow paralyzing fear a home in your psyche, you eliminate one barrier and ease the effects of these changes. They may slow your movement forward or add a detour, but once you transcend these challenges and move beyond your fear, your resolve is strengthened.

13. **Learn to embrace change** This skill is necessary for progressive movement forward. Change is what you expect because you're letting go of attitudes and habits that don't work while adopting and adjusting to new methods. By resisting called-for changes in habits, you're working behind barriers to goal achievement. Some of your goals are short-term and others require more time. Short-term goals are usually achieved with proven skills and habits you already have. Achieving long-term goals requires sustained change and the addition of new skills. Constantly reject the old habits.

14. **Always ask questions of people you trust, those who are authorities in the areas you need answers.** You don't have all the

answers. If you do, please pass this manual to someone else.

15. **Learn to use language that transforms your thinking and fosters courage and confidence to move forward.** Transformative language is not infused with phrases that limit or reduce personal responsibility such as, "If I have time, I will . . ." "I may go depending on . . ." "Only if the weather permits . . ." With this type of language you limit forward movement. Try, "I have fifteen minutes before class to review my notes." "I'll take my umbrella in case it rains." You did not erect any barriers in this approach to time management or if the weather changes. You are prepared to act beyond the challenges of uncertain weather and time constraints. Constantly question yourself. "What do I need to reach goal?" "What resources do I have?" "What additional resources do I need?" The answers expand your opportunities.

16. **Strengthen your listening skills.** The reason you listen is to obtain information on which to act and convey empathy with the speaker. You are constantly making decisions as you move toward your goals; therefore be open to obtaining information from all available sources. Listening to others is one of the sources that may provide additional information for increased opportunities.

17. **Develop the will to go that extra mile.** If you set weekly, bi-weekly or monthly

timelines for completing small goals or steps, you have a built-in mechanism motivating you to continue moving, thereby avoiding procrastination.

18. **Review your progress when the road gets rough.** A review will highlight weaknesses such as inadequate information or resources. It refreshes your efforts, determination and motivation. You find lessons such as avoiding snap judgments about people, seeking professional help as needed or taking time to acquire additional knowledge. This process also reduces stress and uncertainty whether you're moving in the right direction.

19. **Understand the importance of keeping your team involved.** This maximizes the team's effectiveness. You get feedback from people you trust who have information and expertise about your goal. It is wise to include people who are not afraid to offer corrections. Each member contributes a special talent. That talent should fit within your plan like the piece of a puzzle.

20. **Learn to rely on facts, not only on your feelings and emotions that can be weighted with fear or unreasonable biases.** By relying on facts you reach conclusions based in truth rather than decisions filtered through biased emotions. You may need information and seek it from someone who reminds you of a treasured childhood friend or who uses phrases your mother used. Because of these

memories you may be overly persuaded this person has useful information or is right for your team. Facts may demonstrate she has no reliable information and is not suitable for the team.

21. **Develop the courage to enjoy every step of your journey even in the face of disappointment.** Building courage starts with overcoming small fears. You have prepared a solid plan for movement forward and allowed space for alternatives and changes. This plan is a bulwark against doubt and fear by providing small progressive steps, a process of review and direction for acquiring additional resources and information.

22. **Learn to minimalize.** Get the most from even the least amount of resources available to you, especially when allocating time resources. This skill concentrates your focus. Get rid of the attitude, "I could do this, if only I had . . ." or "My journey would be easier, if only my spouse would . . ." or "I could complete this assignment, if only . . ." or "I could exercise today, if only . . ." Your wait for the, "if onlys," in life is a trap. This is another form of procrastination. Stop stalling.

23. **Learn to trust your instincts and first impressions.** If they have been reliable predictors of results in the past, they will be valuable assets during your journey to goal.

24. **Be willing to correct mistakes immediately.** If you don't, they become a drag on progress, slow movement forward and possibly lead you in a direction away from your goal.

25. **Learn to let go of those aspects and issues that come into your life over which you have no control.** They are usually the actions and behaviors of other people: your children, siblings, cousins, dear friends, colleagues—all of them people you love unconditionally. This is difficult because their lives are entwined with yours. They make up an immense part of your identity. When they make faulty decisions then come to you for solutions, refuse to accept their burdens and attempts to transfer the negative consequences of their decisions to you. They will come to you a second, third and fourth time. Continue to say no if they are not in emergency, life-threatening or critical situations requiring your immediate assistance.

26. **Recognize the importance of learning stress-reduction techniques.** Stress interferes with your ability to focus and may affect how you interpret and process information. Stressors are distractions.

27. **Understand the necessity of challenging your assumptions at times during your journey.** If you need to add or delete steps then it may be appropriate to review initial assumptions underlying your plan

or particular parts of the plan. Does your assumption regarding time available need to be revised? Did one of your individual resources disappear? Your cousin who promised to help with renovations married and moved out of state. What is the impact on your assumption of his help in your budding home improvement business?

28. **Understand new circumstances may require new interpretations.** How you interpret circumstances in one situation may not be appropriate in a new or different situation. If you are in a time of financial challenge, cut expenses. When this issue is resolved keep expenses in check, but not to the detriment of spending for a new heating system or other emergency repair. Under the former circumstance, your interpretation to cut spending was correct. But when your heating system died, not spending for a new one is a wrong interpretation.

29. **Overcome any reluctance you have to take ownership of your goals and dreams.** A major aspect of ownership is maintenance. As with any material object you own (house, car, lawnmower, vacuum cleaner or air conditioner), your goals and dreams must also be maintained. If not, their value is reduced and ultimately rendered worthless. Compare the maintenance of a car with maintaining your goal or dream. Just as a car is what it purports to be—a vehicle for

transportation—your goal represents who you are, your hopes, aspirations and history. Keep your car on a regular maintenance schedule. Continue to review and adjust the plan for your goal as necessary. With your car you're always making judgments about little noises and hesitations—the meaning of that pinging sound or the engine hesitation at traffic stops. With the goal you're always assessing the appropriateness of various steps in your plan. When your car needs repairs, they must be done if the car is to remain roadworthy. With your goals and dreams, it's important to correct errors immediately, eliminate unproductive aspects of the plan and gather additional information. Another aspect of ownership is owning your circumstances: the good times and the challenging. You can't claim ownership of certain parts of your life and reject the remainder. Journey to goal requires you own the total package. This attribute provides a historical record of lessons for future use.

30. **Learn to avoid erecting barriers to opportunities by letting go of grudges, biases, prejudices and labels.** When you retain your anger or hold onto a grudge against someone, you reduce focus on your goal. So it is with prejudice and bias.

31. **Practice patience.** Practicing patience assures you're moving forward by walking in the truth of your purpose. Patience

fosters trust in your goal and the plan you made. It broadens your view of the journey by providing opportunities for smoothing bumps and avoiding potholes. Also, you have additional time to absorb lessons learned and internalize changes made. Patience permits growth in confidence that you are moving toward goal achievement. When you are patiently developing new skills, you're likely to avoid costly mistakes.

<u>Focus</u>

Look down the road, what do I see
My love, my dream in front of me
I ask myself, how can it be
I own this dream, not he or she

Focus is the ability to shut out all things unrelated to the object of your attention. However it is not tunnel vision preventing you from considering anything outside the confines of the tunnel. It is intense concentration from which you receive feedback via sensory cues. With focus you're never ambivalent about your goal. Ambivalence steals time available for goal completion. There may be a detour or two for good cause, but the compass always points to goal.

Focus intently on the end game, and then back into your present position. The next step is there waiting for action. Don't hesitate. Make the move. When you're focused you feed a hunger for goal achievement that must be satisfied. Determination to satisfy this hunger keeps your focus on the goal, developing and strengthening skills necessary for forward movement. You're learning to rein in scattered thoughts and actions.

Your focus on goal should be girded by facts supporting your expectations, not emotions. Focus opens your mind to developing each opportunity that presents itself. But focus and action must never be disconnected from justice and empathy for others. Using people to get your objective is not focus, but faulty intentions leading to instability. As you focus on your goal,

> Focus combines concentration, creativity and action.

beware of circumstances that appear to need immediate attention. While they may be important, attention to them diverts focus from goal achievement.

Keep a laser-like beam on your goal

Distractions often hijack focus and weaken commitment. The connection between your brain and the path to your goal must remain unbroken. Keep your mind on that point where your imagination and expectations converge. Direct your attention to the specific outcome you want and channel your energy toward that end. When you combine focus and energy, you are positioned to take giant steps forward. If they don't work together, you end up spinning wheels and moving in circles.

With focus, you avoid procrastination because the steps to your goal are always in sight. Even with the goal never far from your thoughts, remember the importance of balancing other aspects of your life:

family, work, leisure and community activities. An unbalanced lifestyle is a distraction on your journey to goal.

You will be challenged by distractions. They slow your progress as long as you permit their intrusions. No matter your attempts to focus on goal-actions, your mind constantly returns to some other project. If it is a barrier to your continued forward movement, then make a decision and handle the issue. If it's not an emergency, leave it for another time. The problem is your unwillingness to make a decision. This is procrastination. Until you decide how you'll address this other nagging situation, you're unable to focus on your goal. The key to meeting and rising above the challenge is to immediately return to your plan once you've handled the matter according to its importance. Do not use the distraction as an opportunity for procrastination. There will be many other distractions. Some masquerade as important endeavors when in fact they are simply sidelining your efforts. Knowing the difference between acting on these distractions and staying true to the steps in your plan requires you to recognize patterns of procrastination. Remember procrastination is a dream killer.

> Change presents new opportunities— Embrace them

Anticipate particular problems that may arise

In the process of directing your focus, you are in the best position to anticipate issues needing attention because of the plan you made. You're positioned to make appropriate adjustments for addressing these situations. Learn to take care of issues, challenges or problems that, if put on the back burner, may derail your progress.

> Avoid circular thinking–
> It's a barrier to progress

Consider an example you may have experienced. You make a decision to declutter the bedroom. The first chore is to remove clothes from the backs of chairs and put them away. Instead you take the week's newspapers from the floor for placement in the recycle bin. In route your attention is drawn to papers and mail piled on the floor in another room, you stop and begin to sort them. Thirty minutes later you're still trying to find a place for the magazines to keep. By the time this chore is well underway, the bedroom is still messy, newspapers are now on the floor of an adjacent room and there are five to six piles of mail and magazines that have also landed on the floor. Your focus on the bedroom disappeared. The room is still cluttered while you wasted time simply moving things around. Distractions hijacked your goal. Of course if you have domestic help, this chore is greatly reduced or eliminated.

Today, your life is likely to be in constant motion. The world clamors for your attention; family, friends, colleagues, even strangers, cell phones, other electronic devices and ads call out to you from sidewalk billboards. Giant pictures on walls entice you to consider this product or that service. Often the siren calls of these messages are subtle. Even as your mental computer digests a particular message, there is another and still another. These calls for your attention may become distractions as you pursue your plan for goal achievement.

> Focus eliminates distractions

However, commitment and focus on goal blunt the extraneous messages.

Getting closer to the goal frees your mind for more empowering thoughts leading to acts and changes necessary for goal achievement. Moving forward, your new habits are noticed by others and interaction with them becomes more positive. Be kind, respectful and willing to encourage those you encounter. It's like a ripple in a stream; good words and actions spread.

Factoring in the practical skills you currently possess gives a powerful boost to your focus capability. These are skills you've perfected and don't need to think about, such as the habit of arriving for an appointment on time so you're not stressed with fear of being late. If your goal is to run a marathon and you currently run six miles each day, then you've developed the skill of pacing yourself. Take this skill with you as you train for the marathon. As a teenager you helped your mother prepare food for church suppers and fundraisers in the community. Now your goal is to open a catering business. Your previous skills of estimating the number of people to be served, shopping for food, getting the best prices and preparing food are skills you've already developed. They can now be transferred to the catering business. With these skills, you act instinctively. Even infants have practical skills. They learn how to pitch their cries to summon adults, know which cry will get them lifted from their cribs and which cry signals a diaper change is needed.

Focus makes it easier to spot mistakes and will move you forward despite challenges. It fosters boldness in support of your struggles by concentrating attention on the goal. At times when it is difficult to focus on your dream or goal, try concentrating on the implementation of one of the smaller steps in the plan. When you're focused, you stretch yourself by seeing possibilities beyond your horizons.

Begin each day with the purpose of successful goal completion firmly centered in your mind. Remember, today is tomorrow's yesterday. Every day counts. What you do today forms the foundation for tomorrow's actions.

Specific suggestions that tighten your focus

1. **Know your goal is authentic.** Be absolutely sure the goal is a representation of your true self, the values you hold dear and the reasons for pursuit of the goal. Your system of values embodies the principles by which you live

and they are resources and supports for the goal. Authenticity equals truth. Any actions you undertake outside the truth of who you are, will lead away from the goal. If your goal is to purchase a home, car or another important item, the ability to pay for it must be based on your current income minus expenses. If you attempt the purchase on income alone, expenses you choose to ignore will act as barriers to goal achievement. You're not acting in truth. If, however, you have other assets available, your purchasing power is expanded. Suppose you are an introverted type who enjoys quiet time alone or in small groups and someone convinces you to campaign for political office. If you accept, can you stand the constant required interaction with so many people? Are you acting in truth? Your answers determine whether you move forward. Only act in truth with boldness, tenacity and courage.

2. **Learn to reduce and eliminate distractions** by keeping a clear vision of the goal prominent in your thoughts. Distractions only live if you feed into them. They have no power without your consent.

3. **Protect your time** by budgeting it wisely so all necessary actions are included in logical and progressive order. Time keeps moving forward; don't let it leave you behind.

4. **Learn to manage the pursuit of your goal against exaggerated needs of others.** This

is tricky. Be alert for the guilt trips thrown at you, the hurt feelings or the you-owe-me-attitude of others. When you recognize these villains, you can protect yourself by saying no and meaning no.

5. **Concentrate on your strengths.** They provide built-in skills you already have and much of the foundation for your goal attainment. Examine past successes and note the attributes that made you successful in each instance. They are skills that can be replicated in pursuit of your current goals. You will surely recognize the importance focus played in those successes.

6. **Learn to use the resources you have.** We tend to think more is better. That may be true when more information is needed. It's important to get every ounce of value from all resources you currently have available. Recycle and reuse these resources.

7. **Learn to be diligent in monitoring your thinking for protection against unreasonable fear.** Succumbing to fear weakens your ability to concentrate energy on the goal, thus fracturing your focus, which diminishes all the efforts. Fear further clouds your focus by casting a shadow on or building a barrier between you and the goal.

8. **Learn to guard against procrastination, lies, confusion, excuses and negative self-talk.** They derail your efforts. While your attention is dominated by one of these other

issues, you're losing focus on your goal. You're now dallying with unimportant tasks instead of performing the steps set forth in your plan.

9. **Know the value of constant examination and observation of changes** taking place and you'll know if you're making choices that move you forward or call for corrective action. To know the difference, determine, whether your choices follow the steps in your plan. Your decision to make a change or continue in the same direction depends on your answer. When changes begin you become aware of small habits that previously slipped your notice. Many of these habits are hidden saboteurs to the success of goal achievement. Example. My preference is to begin writing early in the day, but the habits of relaxing with a mug of coffee, watching the sun rise and catching up on world news events often delay the start of my writing. While these small indulgences form the foundation of my optimistic outlook for the day, they can thwart my early morning writing plans. I'm then susceptible to the intrusion of phone calls or other distractions that interfere with my writing schedule.

10. **Stay alert for hidden barriers that are not always obvious.** They can hide behind normal everyday existence. They are erected by past experiences, biases, nurturing, trust, education, methods you learned to use

in resolving issues of conflict and strong emotional needs. One of these barriers you don't recognize may be limiting your efforts and progress. Consider this situation. You're saving for a special vacation. For the last two years you dedicated a specific sum each month toward the planned trip. Your best friend asks you to support her organization by purchasing tickets for an annual social event. Immediately you experience contrasting emotions; your strong emotional need to support your friend, weighed against the desire to continue depositing funds into the vacation account. Fear of her disapproval if you say no can become a barrier to your disciplined savings for the trip, by introducing ambiguity into the plan.

11. **Clear away physical distractions in your environment**—unnecessary noise, clutter and, sometimes, people.

12. **Learn to release the distractions of toxic emotions.** Extreme anger, prolonged sadness, unexplained anxiety and unreasonable fears are emotions that likely demand professional intervention. Ignoring these emotions, not only interferes with goal fulfillment, but adversely impacts your health. The first time you confront your fear, anxiety or prolonged sadness will be the hardest. However as you continue moving forward, your efforts to overcome them will become stronger. Also

release yourself from toxic people by putting space between you and them.

13. **Learn to reduce stressors.** They are distractions that concentrate your focus on what might or might not happen at sometime in the future.

14. **Recognize procrastination in all its disguises.** There are many ways you procrastinate: over-scheduling, waiting until the last minute, delaying decision making, lying to yourself about the true nature of your time and resources, permitting others to hand over their problems to you; grandiose and magical thinking; inertia; giving into unreasonable fears; certain cultural references; delaying acquisition of additional information; succumbing to daydreaming instead of taking action on your plan; getting stuck on one step in the plan; ambivalent behavior; creeping inactivity and any other action that takes your mind too long from goal attainment. If you don't have an authentic answer for why you aren't acting on your plan, then you're procrastinating.

15. **Concentrate on present actions.** Commit to completing the task in front of you before moving to another. This habit strengthens your ability to focus.

16. **Understand you always keep your attention on possibilities not limitations.** Concentrating on possibilities strengthens focus by overcoming fearful thoughts. You're

learning to consider avenues beyond your previous conceptions of possibilities.

17. **Recognize actions in pursuit of your goal must have a minimum time-set every day.** Because of commitments such as work, family, public service and other life requirements, assign a minimum amount of time daily for your goal pursuit. Ruthlessly adhere to the time you select.

18. **Learn to use associations.** Practice associating your actions with goal achievement. For example. If you're saving for the purchase of a home, then every saving event should mentally be associated with the down payment. If you need to lose twenty pounds, associate a daily walk with goal pursuit. To improve your chance for becoming debt free, associate every payment on your credit card with the knowledge you are developing appropriate money management habits. As you build and reinforce positive associations, negative associations begin to lose power and disappear.

<u>Discipline</u>

The lazy man, his time, he wastes
As years go by, he cuts and pastes
His dreams, they die, but not in haste
They drip away, with bitter taste

Discipline builds strength and endurance. It is the natural outcome of commitment and the glue that holds all your efforts together. Discipline establishes firm habits and brings order to the actions you take. It is only through discipline that habits are learned, reinforced and become your reality. Therefore, changing unproductive or slack habits takes great courage and effort. Bad habits never lead to goal attainment, but to disaster as they become more entrenched with their frequency of use. They develop power, therefore, when you try to save money, get out of debt, lose weight, change thought patterns, bad habits tend to act independently sabotaging your efforts. Disciplined action is the only method that strengthens new habits. The power of your brain supports your efforts by establishing neural connections carrying more empowering messages that reinforce these new habits.

By folding discipline into commitment you create a self-fulfilling process for success. At age seven I became infatuated with the graceful majorettes who marched in parades. Bands with majorettes were big in the high schools of my childhood. I was not old enough to participate, however I was there for all parades and closely observed the beauty of the short silk skirts, white boots and spinning batons. My desire to be a part of this esteemed group was intense. With the baton my mother purchased for me, I began to learn the basics. Staying after school and practicing with other girls, I honed my technique. As a fifth grader I was permitted to join the junior majorettes. Our uniforms were green silk. It was thrilling. In junior high school I became a "real" majorette attached to the school band. My goal was now expanded. I wanted to become the "solo twirler." This position was always held by a twelfth-grade girl with the highest skill level. I practiced at home and stayed after school building my skills. The disciplined habit of practicing everyday increased my twirling skills, stamina, the ability to adopt new routines and create a few routines of my own. I could confidently catch the baton behind my back and under my knees while marching. Each year I strengthened and expanded these skills knowing I had to be the best. Now you see where I'm going with this. I set a **goal** and observed others who had reached the top in this

> Act in truth with boldness, tenacity and courage

endeavor. I made a **commitment** to do whatever was necessary to reach this goal. I **disciplined** myself to practice every day and take advantage of all opportunities. The head majorette at the University of Miami held clinics at my high school and I participated. During summer vacations I carried my baton and practiced twirling techniques. My goal was clear, my

> Working hard and doing your best still counts

commitment never wavered and I maintained a twenty-twenty **focus** on becoming the number one majorette. Of course there was a decision maker in this process, but I observed over the years that only the most skilled girl was selected. I **persevered** and was chosen. To this day, whenever I set a goal I recall my journey to become solo twirler and review the natural progression to goal fulfillment. It started with a **plan** in the second grade to take all required steps to move forward. At that stage in my life I didn't understand the process of goal achievement, but being so passionate I continued to observe and internalize what was necessary to capture the position, never permitting any self-imposed barriers to interfere with my focus. This is the same process I've observed used by other goal achievers.

Once you set out to achieve your goal, it is my belief; discipline is the most important aspect of success. Discipline moves you forward by forcing action even when you're distracted by day to day activities. It becomes a strong motivator and vital part of your daily life. Discipline must become your master. If you are not disciplined, distractions weaken and ultimately rob you of your dreams.

Establish habits that strengthen your efforts

Consistency of efforts and actions produce results because actions you perform

> Your choice today is your law tomorrow

continuously evolve into habits you are capable of doing automatically. Habits are formed over time and are usually attached to specific goals, but have the power to expand all your horizons. These repeated efforts and actions ease your move along the journey to goal and tend to reflect your personal expectations. Therefore, good habits or bad, keep you captive. The challenge is to make sure the habits you establish keep moving you toward goal achievement. Introduce one small new and positive habit and you experience profound changes. Habits are also attached to emotions: therefore they can hold you hostage in an outdated sense of security or comfort such as the habit of avoiding any type of risk, which limits your possibilities. Another habit that slows goal achievement is delaying today's action until tomorrow. This is procrastination.

Productive habits may be replicated in other aspects of your life. Your decisions and actions to work every workday, arrive on time and perform required duties are habits you don't need to think about when your goal is a paycheck. This consistency assures job retention and all benefits that inure to you through the employment. You only rid yourself of negative or unproductive habits by doggedly persevering with the introduction of new habits. Be courageous even when gripped by fear.

This often requires movement outside your comfort zone. Ask anyone who has tried to quit smoking, lose twenty pounds, get out

> Understand and weigh consequences, they matter

of debt or save money. The old habits of taking a puff, eating two doughnuts, charging that special blouse or living paycheck to paycheck have a strong pull on the psyche, thus the behavior. Therefore, you must get up every time you fall back and try again. This allows the new habit to take hold and gradually establish itself. Soon the new habit will supplant that old tired way of thinking and behaving. Sometimes unproductive habits are so ingrained you may need professional help to make necessary changes. If you need it, get help.

Shedding out-dated habits as you establish new ones puts you in an overlapping zone covering the old behavior as well as the new. This is a tough place to be because the strong pull of old habits will not let go easily. They are stronger because they're established in your mind. You're pulled in two directions. But hold onto your pursuit of change by taking small steps forward in the new direction or by standing still for a time, not letting the sting of doubt steal your motivation. Your small efforts with consistency become a force of power that eventually destroys unproductive habits.

As you strengthen new positive habits, let go of grudges and negativity. They consume too much energy. Your energy is needed for goal achievement. Nursing grudges hampers your efforts. You are permitting someone or some other force to slow or steal your momentum. These ancillary matters have now become self-imposed barriers.

> Skills, like muscles, become stronger with use

Meanwhile, don't let the actions of others derail the journey to goal attainment. Attending to their requirements when necessary, may temporarily slow your actions, but do what you are able until you can again focus on your own plans. An example is your goal to lose weight, but your boss/supervisor/principal/chief requests your attendance at an early morning meeting and you can't walk or exercise before starting work. As an alternative, try walking during lunch. If that time is unavailable, don't be hard on yourself. Return to your exercise regimen the following morning.

If you bump into a financial challenge with your weekly savings goal and are unable to save $100.00 this week, then save $25.00 or even $10.00. The important point is to save something, however small. Even depositing a smaller amount moves you forward and reinforces the discipline of weekly saving. Any movement towards your goal adds big gains on the road to financial stability. The skill to develop and strengthen is the weekly savings habit.

Once a new habit is established you can never go back to the previous unproductive behavior as long as you continue using only those attributes and behaviors that support the new habits. You are on a higher level with the opportunity to move to the next level, closer to your goal.

> Multiply the power of thank you

Predictability

When you are disciplined in pursuing your goals, you're in a position to predict challenges, slowdowns, bumps and potholes that may be in front of you. Success remains attainable because you're following the steps in your plan. Acting on these steps sharpens your skills and reduces fear of moving to the next level. The energy of your disciplined actions and expectations feed on each other and naturally produce successful movement.

Change

Discipline forces change. Expect it. Change is a dynamic always in motion with the power to transform your behavior. It fosters growth. There will be changes that arrive in your life uninvited. Use those aspects of change that move you forward and learn to avoid or repel those that are not useful. On the road of change, you'll surely confront one of those potholes I warned you about earlier. It could be a relative who drops a family problem at your feet. An unfortunate financial issue overtakes your efforts. A health challenge rises to suck the energy from your efforts. A love-one disappoints.

> Discipline forces change

This is the time to put up a fight. Resist the desire to give in and abandon your dream. Stand bold as the strong winds of circumstance swirl around you. Keep the dream safe in a protected place, locked in your mind, away from negativity. You are changing a system of thinking and living. The structure of your thinking process directs your behavior, which determines whether you meet your goals.

The changes you make may be necessitated by major life transitions, such as moving from youth to young adulthood; onto the middle stage; preparation for retirement and beyond. The current process of making decisions may be at odds with the new methods you've chosen to move your life toward goal. Be alert for the conflict these changes produce between the old and new. The conflict must be resolved by reaching a decision that permits you to move forward in the truth of your own authenticity.

You know you are changing because you're now being buffeted by forces from both sides. Hang on until your behavior tips to the side of change. Then confidently step forward. The hard work necessary at this time eventually pays magnificent dividends. Remember each small step is a giant move forward. Working hard and doing your best still counts, big time. If you are in a situation (employment, family, social, business) and it's difficult to balance your goals and obligations, then review the plan and rearrange steps as necessary to get through the challenge.

Follow-through is the child of discipline

With follow-through, you put yourself in a position for moving to the next level. An example from my literary endeavors: I try disciplining myself with a goal of writing at least five pages a day or performing an activity that moves my project forward. Sometimes I fall short, but at the end of each day I've completed one, two or three pages or reviewing and rewriting passages previously written. I may be at a point in the manuscript where I need to get additional information before finishing a paragraph or chapter. I must follow-through by using the library or doing online research. Following my research, new ideas or areas to explore spark additional creativity. If I don't follow-through with needed research, I'm unable to complete the passage or move to the next section or scene in my plot.

Specific actions, skills, and behaviors that aid discipline

1. **Understand discipline directs and concentrates your efforts,** making them more powerful. Discipline gets things done.

2. **Develop self-motivation by internalizing responsibility for your own actions.** Constantly remind yourself this dream or goal is yours alone; therefore, the actions for achievement are yours to own.

3. **Know that discipline builds confidence in the future.** Because discipline strengthens your efforts, the possibility of success will appear less remote and the vision of the goal clearly in focus.

4. **Establish a sense of independence.** By challenging ideas and processes regularly, you identify those that no longer work. Examine them from different angles. You may need to revise or reject them. Therefore, if an idea or a process becomes outdated, it then weakens progress and destabilizes your disciplined efforts. Make changes.

5. **Develop habits that only move you forward.** The battle to establish this skill-set is between you and yourself. You must dig deep and wrestle to the ground, that inner part of you which stands as a barrier to your success. Fear and procrastination are major culprits. Relentlessly use the new habits. As you reinforce these new habits they become

like iron, strong and hard to break. Every single day you must perform actions that move you toward the goal. Constantly refer to your plan for guidance. The steps outlined in the plan are vital to your success.

6. **Conquer boredom by developing the ability to tolerate above-normal repetition.** Discipline requires repeated actions that may become susceptible to boredom. Continue these disciplined actions while adding small increases as dictated by your plan. You establish the desired new habits.

7. **Keep your focus on the goal.** This encourages continued disciplined actions.

8. **Recognize the necessity of disciplining your thought patterns** just as you did in adopting the habit of disciplined actions. Attitude directs your thoughts, which direct your actions, therefore stay alert for any seepage of negativity. It is poison for goal achievement.

9. **Understand disciplined behavior repels distractions and aids focus.** Condition your mind to believe that absent discipline, your goal can never be achieved.

10. **Understand disciplined action is a calculated risk that gives you a competitive edge.** You have weighed the risk of not taking action against the rewards of goal fulfillment and the scale tilts to the side of goal. Your motivation to continue all disciplined actions becomes stronger.

11. **Confront unworkable habits and ditch them.** You override these bad habits by establishing new ones. When they come upon you, immediately substitute the new habits. There will, however, be one or two well-entrenched habits that seem impossible to change. They creep up on you at unexpected times. When they do, remind yourself you have a new and different way of handling these habits—to make them disappear. You're required to use this narrative many times during your journey before these habits fade into history.

12. **Be prepared when you reach a plateau.** When you seem to be standing still despite all your efforts you're at a plateau. Plateauing is a dangerous time. Your enthusiasm may flatten. During this period you're not receiving the positive feedback you want because your disciplined actions appear not to produce change. Nevertheless you're strengthening new habits. By continued work you gradually move to the next step. Patience is required.

Perseverance, the Mantle of Strength

Get up; go on, this very day
A steady move, is the only way
That dream you made in the Month of May
Comes true, so now you play

With perseverance you persist through the ups and downs of your journey. When you're frightened and battered by circumstances that urge you to give up or turn back to your comfortable reliance on unproductive habits, resist. Go deep within, to your core: there you'll find the fortitude and motivation to keep moving forward. Persuade yourself with encouraging thoughts and words to push on when the goal appears too far away. Remember, the pursuit of your goal is not always easy. The road is sometimes rocky and filled with potholes, but goal achievement demands perseverance. Take one step at a time. When you look back, the starting point is a distant milestone. Even small movement forward fuels your desire for continued and greater successes as you discover additional skills and develop new habits. Perseverance is a lonely, but patient companion. It quietly supports and strengthens every move you make.

When discipline and perseverance intercept, mind and body act as one. Olympic medal winners and other super-performing athletes do not rise to the top of their sports by accident. Their individual decisions result in the disciplined behavior of practicing relentlessly and making skill development a priority. Rain or shine they forge ahead. Their continued actions finally cause their bodies to follow the dictates of their minds. No progress happens without perseverance.

> Perseverance can only be supported by a clear plan

As you persevere, unknown aspects of yourself unfold, revealing hidden powers that will sustain your forward movement with small successes. It may become emotionally painful to keep moving when barriers continue confronting your efforts. By staying the course, step by step, you preserve your progress.

Required attitude

Practice patience as you move along the road toward your goal. It pays substantial rewards. Patience fosters trust in the goal and plan you made and is a close relative of wise use of time. When struggling to change life-long habits that never worked, you will need extra time, which demands patience. It is vital you continue monitoring your progress, making corrections and changes when necessary. If you ignore these steps you'll find yourself having to reverse and correct mistakes, thus squandering valuable time. Be patient and use the time needed. Don't worry that you may not be moving fast enough. Sustained change requires concentrated and deliberate actions over time.

> Fear and doubt cannot survive against perseverance

When you experience a crisis of confidence in your ability to realize the goal; your creativity may suffer. During this rough stretch you can remain tuned to your dream by reviewing the actions you have taken. Go over the completed steps. There is the possibility you'll discover additional methods that link what you have done to what you must do now. Write down these new prospects and follow their leads.

Carry your hope along with patience and the journey becomes easier. Your inner spirit encourages continued movement. That spark of inner spirit is what helped some people survive the horrors of genocide, grinding poverty, being prisoners of war or victims of abuse. These people accessed that special place within and held on until their circumstances improved.

Your pursuit of goal is a journey to change circumstances. How much do you want to succeed? Are you prepared to go that extra mile? Are you ready to delay other desires or pleasures? Are you ready to factor in some measure of risk? These questions must be answered many times during your journey. Honest responses compel you to persevere and they reinforce your focus by removing barriers to continued progress.

To achieve your dream, part of the cost is a measure of risk. Any risk you take must be driven by the truth of who you are. Calculate how much risk you can stand. Do the numbers. To lose those 20, 30, 40, or any specified number of pounds, are you willing to take forty minutes of your twenty-four hours to walk and forgo another activity? Calculate the time. To get out of debt, are you willing to go to the back of your closet and wear a blouse, tie or pair of shoes you bought last year, instead of buying new ones? How much can you save if you wear the old tie, blouse or shoes? Run the numbers. To save money for the purchase of a home, for education, retirement, car purchase or another worthy goal, are you willing to pay yourself first? To open your own business, are you willing to spend extra hours researching the process? Examining the numbers will determine your risk, thereby reducing the fear of considering a new choice.

> When you feel you can't go on, take one more step

Do you think Christopher Columbus took a risk when he decided to pursue his dream of reaching the east by sailing west? Think about the astronaut who first walked on the moon. What about Harriet Tubman, when she broke the law to steer other slaves along the Underground Railroad? Thurgood Marshall, when he stood before the U.S. Supreme Court and argued the illegality of the long-held concept of separate but equal; think he took a risk? What about Jackie Robinson? He risked hate speech, physical harm and threats to his life. Was his pursuit of a baseball career a risk? The courageous women who fought conven- tional culture to win

> Perseverance is free. Use as much as you need

voting rights for all women risked their lives. Our great country was born as a result of men who decided to risk war with England. They risked their lives and the lives of their families for the goal of creating a country where individual effort counts.

Change is inevitable as you persevere, expect it. Your goal has lived with you a long time, while huge changes are occurring throughout the world. You need to recognize some of these changes; globalization, healthcare access and costs, retirement options, access to higher education, the meaning of work, the conduct of relationships and every aspect of communications. Many or all of these twenty-first century life-events may affect your goal achievement.

As you persevere to goal, take care of your connections with others. These connections give your life meaning as a reminder you matter. They are important, especially to your emotional peace. Connections to others support your efforts by linking you to the benefits and resources of your culture and social communities. They connect you to the best of your past and future possibilities. You are constantly reminded of the importance of connectedness. There are few places where you don't see people constantly talking on cell phones or using other personal devices that link them to family, friends, acquaintances or important business contacts. There is a feeling of safety knowing another person cares enough to share your life. Connectedness is a necessary element in every part of existence. You, therefore, must also connect your varied life pieces so they work together. This skill is developed by following the different threads of your life. Eventually, they connect.

You cannot master only one skill and expect to achieve your goal. Each skill supports and complements other skills. If you are using the skills acquired for focus, you're naturally strengthening skills for commitment and perseverance. As you persevere you are mastering all your skills. Connecting these skills keeps focus on goal and expands your ability for taking advantage of all opportunities that come to you. When these combined skills work together, you are on the winning side of your calculated risk. Your resolve is stronger.

Specific steps to perseverance

1. **Learn to adapt to changing conditions and circumstances.** Your plan has prepared you to expect change. Stress-reduction skills are assisting you in addressing these changes. Because you're relinquishing old habits and

acquiring new more productive habits you experience increased confidence in your ability to meet the challenges of change.

2. **Learn to go the extra mile.** As you persevere the rope that ties together your dream and its realization becomes stronger and straighter. The skills you have acquired tighten their grip on dream fulfillment and your new more productive habits shorten the time between goal and achievement. This is your second wind.

3. **Learn to improvise.** Unfamiliar circumstances may require different methods of interpreting and processing information. With the skills you've added you begin to trust your decision making when improvisation is required.

4. **Hold onto ownership of your dreams.** It is easier to go through the tough times when you own the process. You cannot then blame others for your delay, frustration or failure. Remember blame consumes energy that should be devoted to goal achievement.

5. **Learn to be frugal with resources.** The resources you rely on must last throughout your journey. Pace their use. Be careful not to spend all the money you included in the plan at any particular stage in the journey. These funds must take you to the end. Likewise, use team members as needed. Don't wear them down. Watch your health. Don't overextend yourself. Prioritize your time so little or none

is wasted. These resources are included in your plan as support for the long haul to goal achievement. Maximize and protect these resources.

6. **Learn to layer your skills for the multiplier effect.** The value of one action you take is magnified to act with the power of many actions. You take the specific action of saving a dedicated sum of money each pay period with automatic deposit. This one action increases your savings, awards compound interest, however small, on the total sum and provides positive feedback that you're working toward your goal and the plan you made is succeeding. The process is also powerful with other investments. If you plan to lose twenty pounds, adopt a single specific action, walk one mile each day. This action increases your physical activity, which burns more calories and keeps your focus on the goal. Another result, you become more sensitive to the benefits of healthy living habits. Therefore, a single skill then becomes more powerful with the support of other skills. Learn to stretch these skills. When you do, there is the opportunity for acquiring additional skills. The cycle continues to replicate itself, moving you closer to goal.

7. **Learn to use connectedness.** You have your team. They are positioned to connect you to organizations, institutions and other individuals who can help your forward

movement. You're also connected to personal organizations outside of the team: schools, religious affiliations, fraternal organizations, civic and social groups and voluntary associations. These are valuable resources available to you.

8. **Develop the ability to eliminate distractions.** Maintain a clear vision of your goal, avoid procrastination, use your time efficiently, declutter your physical environment and avoid burdens of other people. You know it's a distraction if it diminishes your focus on goal achievement.

9. **Understand risk and its importance in goal fulfillment.** Your decision to make a dream come true or achieve a specific goal will naturally involve changes in your thinking, thus your actions. Change always involves risk because you are stepping into new and possibly unknown circumstances. Limit fear of risk with the acquisition of relevant information.

10. **Cultivate the ability to quickly go into survival mode when necessary.** Because of rapid changes in the world today, influences beyond your control may affect the survival of your goal-achievement plans. Survival means accelerated decision making. You experience a higher level of alertness that comes with consideration of new ideas, even though you may discard them later. The important effort here is to maintain your

goal. During this time of survival you expend more energy, therefore another reason for staying healthy.

11. **Develop the habit of constantly sifting through the barrage of information** reaching you and selecting only relevant and meaningful information that supports your plan.

12. **Learn to make consequences an essential part of choice.** You may not be able to foresee all consequences, but you recognize those that will occur immediately, such as sharpened focus, more efficient use of time, knowing changes are required and acceptance of personal responsibility for the journey. These positive consequences affirm your choice or point you in a different direction. Every decision you make has a corresponding consequence. The ultimate consequence is success. Therefore every choice you make should lead to your goal.

13. **Know how to combine previously acquired skills at the appropriate time.** As an old saying admonishes, "You don't have to reinvent the wheel." Continue acquiring information and adopting procedures that worked for others who realized their goals. Their methods have already demonstrated success. Don't be afraid to use them.

14. **Recognize the importance of consistency, diligence and persistence working together.** These attributes strengthen all

the other skills. Likewise they strengthen your resiliency and produce a willingness to be patient as you move toward your goal. An example. After years of filing for tax extensions, you establish a goal this year to file your taxes by April 15th. You develop a plan and the first step is to set up a file folder for each class of deductions. As expenses are paid and recorded you place documentation in the appropriate folder. This procedure works monthly, bi-monthly or quarterly. In January you place income statements in a separate folder. Your unwavering commitment grows stronger because you're focused on performing all steps necessary for the April 15th deadline. By the middle of March, a review of the folders indicates whether additional documents are needed. If so, you have time to obtain them. You're now ready to prepare your tax return or provide the material to an accountant.

15. **Recognize the necessity of refreshing the steps in your plan.** You do this by periodically reviewing the lessons and skills you've acquired to the current level, building on and expanding them. This process is also a strong motivator.

16. **Learn to use the tension between fear and risk.** Risk must be calculated to tilt to your advantage. You have relevant information and the necessary skill level. The tension between fear and risk intensifies your focus

by forcing you to choose which side of the scale supports your goal. Example. You establish a goal to resume your education after raising a family, but you fear attending classes with younger students. Weigh the important benefits that come with education against fear of the unknown reactions of these students.

17. **Understand perseverance adds value to your efforts.** Don't permit negativity, fear, lax discipline, actions of others and procrastination to devalue your efforts.

18. **Understand when you tire you can take a break,** but never succumb to the urge to quit. Know the difference. Quitting means you abandon your goal. When taking a break you're recharging your energy.

19. **Learn to get beyond the plateau effect.** Discipline becomes the lead actor at this point in your journey. Continue persevering with the steps in your plan; eventually these actions produce big gains that move you beyond the plateau to the next step. During the plateau you are conditioning and strengthening your skills.

20. **Understand perseverance produces continuous stimulation of your thinking process,** by permeating your behavioral patterns. This causes positive changes in your habits. These changed habits ultimately lead to correct choices for goal achievement. The process is continuous. Every step on the

road to goal must be achieved. A single step cannot succeed alone; all the steps in your plan must work together as a team.

21. **Learn to be resilient.** During the journey you become more resilient as you overcome challenges, barriers and potholes. You're conditioning your mind which strengthens your resolve in moving forward. These successes are motivating forces. They sharpen problem-solving capabilities. The result is more confidence in your ability for finding solutions to future challenges. With these small successes you begin to experience a growing sense of certainty for achievement of your goal.

A Few Final Words

As you continue moving forward with your goals and dreams, be aware globalization shrinks the world and will have a huge impact on how you live your life, make plans and carry them out. Your goals and dreams exist in this complex global environment, therefore your planning cannot proceed without considering the interconnected world. You must demystify its implications in a manner you clearly understand. It affects your finances, health, leisure, communications, housing, education, food consumption, employment, retirement, even how to solve day-to-day challenges. As barriers to global competition fall, opportunities rise if you are bold enough to present your dreams and goals to the world.

Because you interact with people around the globe, you need to understand cultural idioms, idiosyncrasies and what your actions may represent to someone of a different culture. This understanding will guide you when goal attainment involves aspects of an unfamiliar culture and possibly prevent problems or smooth your path. This is especially true if your goal involves commerce.

Globalization impacts how we interpret the meaning of work in this century, who will work, the kind of work they'll do and the knowledge, education and skills required. Like so many of us today you may still think of work as a brick and mortar destination where you perform a function for compensation. This compensation package usually includes benefits such as sick leave, vacation time, health insurance, retirement and other employee services. These benefits, however, are quickly shrinking or being severely curtailed. There are jobs which have disappeared and will never return. This reality may affect the success of your dream. It is, therefore, imperative that you understand how the global workplace may dictate your individual ability to work or sustain employment. Anticipating bumps and potholes ahead, you must ask these questions. How long will the services I provide be needed? Can a computer perform my job? Can my job be done more cheaply in another part of the world? Are my skills up to date? Do I have enough education? Will this job maintain my living standard? Is this job an asset that will increase in value or is its value destined to decline in the future? Are my skills interchangeable? Can my dream survive with the skills I have? You need to have answers. Even professions that have been considered sacrosanct are changing. Today, teachers, law enforcement officers and other public service employees are being laid off and having their benefits cut. Attorneys who once practiced solo are a dying breed. So is the medical doctor who proudly held the title, general practitioner. When is the last time you heard that term? If you are competing for a job with someone in Sarajevo, Mumbai, Helsinki or Rio de Janeiro, how do your skills stack up with those competitors?

Remember computer programming, the excitement of its potential? It can be done anywhere on the globe. On the other hand, HVAC skills will not be out-sourced in the immediate future. But even that may change when we move to green energy. Therefore, pay attention to what is happening in the work world as impacted by globalization. Maybe you don't need to think of a job as being employed by some entity. Your own small business may be what is required to meet your needs and goals. Even then you must be prepared to compete globally. Not only are you competing with the services you offer, you are competing against the networks of transnational groups for whom borders don't exist. They offer their skills and services anywhere.

When you set goals for your work life, anticipate changes you must make. Certain aspects of your work life, be it as a salaried employee, employer, professional, para-professional, solo worker or service provider will change. Globalization also alters where you earn your income. Because you compete with people living half a world away, perhaps you may need to pack your skills and follow your job or trade to another country. Multinational corporations have options to hire employees anywhere in the world. Consider your language capability. One powerful skill is the ability for bilingual communication. Are you motivated to learn another language? You are competing with multilingual people. Can your language skills compete with theirs? Weigh your chances.

Across the globe there are escalating conflicts as world-wide systems shift, alter and sometimes completely collapse. These conflicts breed uncertainty and fear. It is difficult to think of any part of life that will not be affected by this new interconnected global structure. Are you bold enough to navigate one of these potholes on your journey to goal?

Expect to see a rise in the use of symbolism and coded speech as a substitute for facts. Symbols and codes are meant to persuade by tying together seemingly disparate elements that suggest they are interchangeable, thus one standing for the other. They may encompass ideas, belief systems, objects or codes of conduct. Will you take the necessary steps to obtain information needed for interpreting codes and symbols you encounter on your journey?

A symbol exists when one object stands in the place of another different object, idea, belief or principle. Speech may be encoded by the way words are strung together. Code words and symbols may appear to be familiar. When they're transmitted, they reveal their true meaning to those certain people who know how to decipher them. Therefore, the code words you hear may affect your goal, but if you are unable to decode them, you lose ground, because you don't have enough information for decision making. It is essential you learn how to decode these words and symbols tossed at you by people who purport to provide information for your benefit. Are they speaking truth? Did they leave out or distort facts you need to make an appropriate decision? Is the information rhetoric that merely entertains? Is the information meant to change your view to a point you don't understand or know how to question? Are the facts presented authentic? Knowing the difference may impact your plans and ultimately whether you achieve your goal. Understand the language and you will recognize coded speech. Code words and phrases are also used to shorten your consideration of a matter and persuade you to accept the user's definition, outlook, conclusion or meaning conveyed. They can be manipulative. Coded speech is used masterfully by those who market products to you. They urge your acceptance and immediate identification with their points of view, possibly mere propaganda. Accept these code words only if you understand their true meaning and they align with your goal attainment.

Navigating healthcare is another challenge in your journey. It has become a major cost for everyone. How to solve this problem is still under discussion by people who determine cost. So that you will not be eaten alive by these expenses, practice good health habits by eating appropriately, exercising, managing stress and keeping appointments with medical providers. Currently there are employers who still bear most of the costs of healthcare, but that benefit is disappearing. Understanding the new ramifications of healthcare is a must. Perseverance in goal pursuit is difficult if you have a health challenge and cannot access healthcare.

Retirement is another major change that may impact goal achievement. This concept is not even a hundred years old. Retirement is a twentieth-century idea that established itself worldwide. But losing ground are the days when you can look forward to working with one employer for twenty, twenty-five or thirty years, after which you're eligible to retire in your mid-sixties—sometimes earlier—and receive generous benefits for the remainder of your life. That system was fine for its time because it was in line with the actuarial life span. Today the calculated life span has been extended by medical improvements, reduction in infant mortality and improved health conditions, therefore it is likely you will enjoy a longer life. Policy makers are considering expanding the retirement age to align it with current life expectancy. Will this affect your goal to retire early? Who will fund your retirement, you or an employer? That burden is shifting at the speed of light to you. Factor this new reality into the success of your goal attainment. During your lifetime you'll have many work opportunities; therefore you need to understand the options, processes and vehicles available for the goal of successful retirement.

Lack of education is a deal breaker. There is little chance you will move forward without acquiring education and skills you can use in more than a single academic area, job, trade or profession.

Online skills are necessary today. Most employment applications must be completed and submitted online. Education is now available online and the schools providing this type of study are growing exponentially. Even medical professionals can now provide certain of their services through the Internet. Relationships today often begin in cyber space. For sure, much of the interactions between people take place online or via other personal electronic devices. This may be scary and stressful, but it is just one more factor to be considered as you proceed to goal.

As you're moving to achieve your goals, there may come a time you feel the rules are too tough; however quitting is not an option. Life owes you nothing, therefore feeling sorry for yourself, should last no more than a minute. When you begin to think you're owed something, you're then shifting responsibility and action for your goals to someone else who may not be interested in taking on the burden of your existence. Therefore, when you encounter the over-powering urge to give up, throw in the towel or just walk away, gently tell yourself; I am doing my best. But be sure you can honestly say this. The attitude to retreat from your goal may temporarily relieve your stress; however you must take another step. This is also an opportunity to speak encouraging words to yourself. Don't hesitate if you need to see a professional for help in processing the emotions you're experiencing. During these rough days and hard times keep moving, sometimes only by putting one foot in front of the other. Move. Keep going, there is no alternative. In time, you'll be closer to your goal than the day you began. The key is movement, however small. If a time comes when physical movement is just not feasible, then keep your mind moving until you can again physically advance. Never stop.

Once again, go deep into your inner self and latch onto the momentum that brought you to this present point. Stick to the plan. Don't let boredom and weariness steal your dreams. As you go forward, learn to boost and motivate yourself. Develop your intuition. Be bold. Be resourceful. Follow through, but know when to make changes. Just don't abandon your goal when frustration or disappointment interrupts your journey.

The hardest part of your journey is when you're changing from familiar ingrained habits and adopting new more productive habits. It is important at this time that you don't sit and sulk or blame others. Remind yourself you are responsible for your progress.

Dreams have deep roots, thus power. Their tentacles cross generations. Examine the actions of your family. There are lessons in your personal history that will strengthen your skills. The dreams of my own family have come true. My grandfather, Noble R. Williams, Sr., born in Leon County, near Tallahassee, Florida in 1890, dreamed of a better life for himself. To realize his dream he needed to relocate. At a young age he left his home and walked 182 miles to St. Augustine, Florida where he hopped a ride on a freighter headed to Miami. Imagine walking through thick forests, brush, around and sometimes through waterways. Today it would take approximately three hours to drive this distance. I can only imagine how difficult it must have been for him. Did he travel alone? How did he find food, shelter himself during the nights and from the rain? Once he arrived at the coast and found a ship willing to take him, where did they allow him to sit and sleep? These were close to life and death decisions for a black man in the early 1900s. But he did not permit fear to side-track his dream. He weighed the risk of following his dream against his dead-end circumstances. He kept the vision for a better life clearly focused in his mind.

When he arrived, Miami was in the mist of fierce development. There were jobs. He staked his claim on one of them, subsequently married and bought a home in which he and my grandmother raised my father and uncle. My grandfather's dream of a better life flowed down the years to me. His dream formed the foundation for my own goals.

I learned six lessons from my grandfather's pursuit of his dream. (1) Establishing a **goal** and having the ability to imagine different circumstances with more desirable outcomes. (2) Making a **plan** for achievement. He heard there were jobs in Miami, Florida. He needed access to those jobs, so he had to get to Miami. Even though it was the dawn of the automobile era he probably had never seen one. His circumstances were such he had no horse or buggy. (If he had, he would have been able to make a living in his home area.) The only option was to walk to the northeast coast of the state and get on a ship sailing to Miami. He knew he could count on there being back-breaking work for a black man one and a half generations out of slavery. (3) He **committed** himself to taking any legal work, save part of his earnings and take advantage of all opportunities to lift himself higher. (4) He **focused** on his plan, earned enough money to marry another struggler, who, with her parents, had left rural north Florida to settle in the boom town. They focused on their dream of possibilities for a better life for themselves and their children. (5) They were **disciplined** in their efforts, working hard and saving enough money to purchase their own home. (6) These two people **persevered**, sent their sons to college and continued to live their lives, adhering to universal laws of cause and effect that eventually led to the fulfillment of their dreams for me and my siblings.

My grandfather had a vision, hoping to establish a place for himself in an expanding city. To make the vision a reality, he acted boldly, courageously and unafraid to relocate to what was then little more than a swamp. His principles worked and they subsequently launched future generations of my ancestors on the Great Migration north, which further expanded the dream for those who came after him. His road to dream fulfillment was shared by other immigrants from north Florida, the Caribbean and nearby South America. The ancestors of my in-laws also acted boldly. At the same time my grandparents were improving their circumstances; my in-laws left their home in the Bahamas and made the perilous journey to Miami. Their dream was also a better life for their children. Their long-ago actions are powerful lessons whenever I encounter a challenge or pothole.

Throughout the history of our country, the dreams of immigrants benefitted their heirs. Those dreams are resources that provide hope, lessons in the importance of struggle, opportunities and staying the course to successful goal attainment.

Opportunities for achieving your goal are around every corner. See that the choices you make when they appear are supportive of your goals and dreams. When you look at the lessons learned from your ancestors/family, also consider the successes of institutions in your communities. Schools and institutions of higher learning, religious institutions, public service and fraternal organizations and businesses offer powerful lessons in goal achievement. Study the skills they employed in meeting their commercial and public service goals. Those skills will be no different than the ones offered in this manual.

Remember

    (1) Every decision you make has a consequence. Will the consequence work for you or limit your options?

    (2) There is order in the universe you can emulate. The same principles that govern nature also hold sway in building a foundation for your goal. You will always reap what you sow. If you plant peas you will not get apples. Orange trees only

bear oranges, never bananas. If you want melons don't plant corn. Tomato seeds never yield onions.

(3) The time lapse between what you desire and its achievement is shortened by your continued disciplined actions.

(4) Protect your assets and resources and they will sustain you to completion of your journey; this includes relationships with others.

(5) If you see the glass half full rather than half empty, then you'll see opportunities and solutions instead of limitations and barriers.

(6) When you encounter a pothole or bump in the road, don't begin the blame game. You are responsible for yourself and your dreams.

(7) Be confident of success based on lessons learned from past experience, education, preparation, the ability to focus on each step of your plan and the courage to anticipate problems that may be ahead.

(8) Make yourself familiar with the words creativity, veracity and integrity. They empower.

(9) Cultivate and grow your sense of self. You do this by honoring truth and clarity in defining who you are. Reject any negative definitions placed on you by others and refuse to allow negative outside forces to direct your behavior.

(10) Don't forget to be grateful you have developed a plan and are moving through the steps toward your goal.

(11) When the going gets rough, don't settle for mediocrity.

(12) Boldly affirm each step you take. You are committing yourself by building on every achievement, no matter how small. Self-affirmation is a way of celebrating small successes and changing a negative belief system.

(13) There may come a time during your journey when you enter survival mode. When that happens you must become more alert and vigilant, assume greater responsibility and obtain additional information, immediately. Twenty-first century life demands you stay close to survival mode because change today is so rapid and profound. Survival requires you live your life in sync with universal laws and truths that don't change, no matter your current circumstances.

(14) Confronting change takes courage. Face fear of change and disable it by examining yourself and the life you're living. You discover your reasons for living by rules that no longer work—that is if you're honest. Truth and clarity provide courage to make necessary changes.

(15) Making a goal /dream come true requires the support of others. Look at your

environment and honestly ask yourself. Who can I count on to stand with me, no matter how steep the road becomes?

(16) Understand change. Positive change transforms thinking, attitude, behavior and finally results. As you change, be prepared for a sense of loss. When this emotion comes, review the lessons learned as you transition to a new way of thinking and viewing the world.

(17) Don't permit rejection by others to short-circuit your sense of goal purpose. Rejection is someone else's view. They see you and your dream from a different perspective. Their opinions should not diminish who you are and what your dream represents. Remain focused on your goal and the sting of rejection will retreat.

(18) Be aware of code words, symbols, superlatives and any other phrases you don't understand. Get informed. You need to be able to decipher these covert messages, because they may stand as roadblocks to your progress.

(19) Information not only answers questions, it diminishes confusion, reduces fear, and disables anxiety.

(20) Time is with you at the start of your journey. It will walk beside you every step of the way if you give it respect. It will slip away if you don't.

(21) Unproductive and slack habits are like viruses; they spread and infect all aspects of your goal pursuit. Destroy them by persisting with the establishment of new and forward-moving habits.

(22) Good planning reduces the habit of lurching from crisis to crisis. You're moving sideways not forward.

(23) Fear of failure is a barrier to creativity and blocks your ability to see opportunities. Examine your fears. Tear them apart. Name them. You then have a concrete entity to confront and dispose of appropriately.

(24) Don't get stuck in the present, remember your plan is forward-looking. Always keep your goal in sight.

(25) There are processes in life that are eternal and constant. There is birth, growth, change, loss and eventually death. Knowing this to be so, you can plan and live your life abundantly with all the confidence needed to obtain your goals.

(26) Socrates didn't lie when he said "Know thyself." When you know who you are, then you will know where you're going. Seek this knowledge early on. You are the sum of your hopes, dreams, history, genetics and of course, your environment.

(27) When you change your attitude about one thing, you discover it is easier to change your attitude about other matters. Attitude

is the root of your behavior. As in nature, if the root of a tree is healthy the tree thrives and continues to grow.

(28) Your thinking process determines your actions. If you think you can reach the goals you set, every action will strengthen your resolve to keep moving forward carrying stronger skills.

Considering all I have said, what happens if your goal remains in the distance? Realize you have not wasted time. You are successful in the skills learned, behavioral changes made and the new thought patterns wired into your brain. They make your life more fruitful, prosperous and peaceful. The dream is still in play.

When the story of your journey is told let the listeners hear of your bold commitment, unfailing discipline and life-altering perseverance. The tale of the plan that focused your soul will say who you are as nothing else.

Notes

I consulted the Oxford English Dictionary, 2nd Edition, Clarendon Press, Oxford: 1989, to get the most extensive overview of the meaning of words defining principles of successful goal achievement that I suggest in this manual. The Oxford English Dictionary provides an exhaustive history of word usage. According to its own description, it is the most authoritative work on words and usage in the English language. Its history of word usage goes back more than 900 years.

Code *5 . . . a word or symbol used as a substitute for the ordinary name of a thing or person, for secrecy or convenience.* Vol. III, p. 428.

Commit *. . . to put together, join, also, to put for safety, give in charge, entrust . . . put forth . . .* Vol. III p. 559.

Courage *4. That quality of mind which shows itself in facing danger without fear or shrinking; bravery, boldness, valour.* Vol. III, p. 1051.

Diligence *1. Constant and earnest effort to accomplish what is undertaken; persistent application and endeavor; industry, assiduity.* Vol. IV, p. 665.

Discipline *1. To subject to discipline . . . to instruct, educate, train . . . more especially, to train to habits of order and subordination; to bring under control.* Vol. IV, p. 735.

Empower *2. To impart or bestow power to an end or for a purpose; to enable, permit.* Vol. V, p. 192.

Focus *5.a. The centre of activity, or area of greatest energy* . . . The first reference to the use of this word is in 1604 . . . *the burning point of a lens or mirror* . . . In its exhaustive examination of the meaning of focus, the Dictionary describes how the word was used in other disciplines, i.e. geometry, optics, acoustics, medicine, theater, photography. In each of these areas focus refers to a specific point of convergence. Vol. V, p. 1127.

Goal *2.a.b . . . The terminal point of a race . . . The object to which effort or ambition is directed; the destination of a . . . journey.* Vol. VI, p. 632.

Integrity *1.b. Something undivided; an integral whole.* Vol. VII, p. 1066.

Persevere *1. To continue steadfastly in a course of action . . . esp. in the face of difficulty or obstacles; to continue staunch or constant . . .* Vol. XI, p. 593.

Plan *I.2. A design according to which things or parts of a thing are, or are to be, arranged; a scheme of arrangement . . . a type of structure . . .* Vol. XI, p. 958.

Skill *6.a.Capability of accomplishing something with precision and certainty; practical knowledge in combination with ability; cleverness, expertness. Also, an ability to perform a function, acquired or learnt with practice . . .* Vol. XV, p. 603.

Succeed *6.a. To follow or come after in the course of events, the sequence of things, the order of development . . . to take place or come into being subsequently.* Vol. XVII, p. 91.

Symbol 2.a. *Something that stands for, represents, or denotes something else (not by exact resemblance, but by vague suggestion, or by some accidental or conventional relation)* . . . Vol. XVII, p. 451.

Tenacious *1.a. Holding together, cohesive; tough; not easily pulled in pieces or broken.* Vol. XVII, p. 763.

Truth II. 5.a. *Conformity with fact; agreement with reality; accuracy, correctness, verity (of statement or thought).* Vol. XVIII, p. 627.

Glossary of Supportive Words and Phrases–Use Them

Affirmation	Discipline	Opportunity
Balance	Dream	Optimism
Believe	Empathy	Options
Best efforts	Empower	Ownership
Boldness	Expectation	Perseverance
Bravery	Fairness	Plan
Can-do	Focus	Preparation
Capability	Forward-looking	Purpose
Change	Hope	Research
Character	Humility	Responsibility
Choices	Improve	Self-knowledge
Clarity	Improvise	Self-motivation
Commitment	Justice	Simplicity
Conceptualize	Joy	Small steps
Confidence	Learn more	Success
Consistency	Mediate	Team
Courage	Mentor	Time
Decisive action	Morality	Truth
Determination	Never stop	Understanding
Development	Now	Visualize

www.ingramcontent.com/pod-product-compliance
Lightning Source LLC
Chambersburg PA
CBHW020536290526
45786CB00002B/907